THE OFFICIAL NOVELISATION

WRITTEN BY
CHRISTIAN FRANCIS

BASED ON THE SCREENPLAY BY
HARRY BROMLEY DAVENPORT
AND
MICHEL PARRY, ROBERT SMITH, IAIN CASSIE, JO ANN KAPLAN

ECHO ON PUBLISHING

CONTENTS

Welcome to the world of XTRO - bizarre, eccentric and with a surprise at every corner.

The film's initial success has evolved into its becoming a cult classic for which I am grateful since its life has been so extended. Thus, it still plays on cable and streaming and is frequently reissued on DVD.

It's exciting that this new novelization by Christian Francis is now in print.

Be afraid.

Harry Bromley Davenport

1. ARRIVAL

The August warmth had almost left for the day, as Sam Phillips and his eight-year-old son, Tony, were intent on enjoying the remaining afternoon as much as they could. Outside the family's holiday cottage, they were hurling a stick back and forth for their overactive canine, one inventively named Dog. A golden retriever who was made of pure excitement with an endlessly wagging tail.

Sam's wife, Rachel, was in a fluster as she came bustling out of the front door. She'd just realised they didn't have enough for dinner, or for tomorrow's breakfast, and she was on her way to the local shops. Living in a remote cottage, though, 'local' meant a five-mile drive to the next town.

She hurried down the stone path, through the gate, and across the gravel drive to their car: a Morris Minor that had seen better days. As she got to it, she repeated the shopping list in her head: bread, bacon, milk, cheese, cigarettes.

With her handbag slung over her shoulder, she glanced back through the fence, where the dog ran a loose circle around Tony, who was laughing as the dog skidded and fumbled after the stick.

"Won't be long," Rachel called out.

"Remember the bacon!" Sam shouted back with a wave.

At the same time, Tony stopped and ran over to the fence to see his mother off.

"And chocolate!" the boy happily added. "Don't forget the chocolate."

With a smile and a nod, Rachel got into the car. It spluttered and coughed before finally starting. A cloud of smoke puffed out of its exhaust, and the car soon rattled down the lane and out of sight.

The father, son, and dog were left to themselves.

"Come on," Sam said, picking up the stick. He was ready to throw it again, but Dog had other ideas. He dropped to his haunches, forgetting they were playing, and proceeded to lick himself.

"Bloody hell, you're doing that *now*?" Sam laughed. "All right, new game," he said to Tony. "Who can throw this stick the highest? You first!"

Tony happily walked over and took the stick, immediately flinging it upward. But with him being so young, the stick spun only ten feet above and quickly dropped to the grass with a dull thud.

"Not bad. Not bad at all," Sam said, mock

impressed. Getting the stick, he weighed it in his hand. "Okay, okay... Now watch this."

Neither of them noticed that Dog had stopped licking himself. Instead, his head was craned skyward, ears pricked up, as a growl rumbled from his throat. His eyes weren't on the stick. They were on what was above.

Sam winked at his son, then threw the stick up as hard as he could. It climbed, spinning higher than the thatch of the cottage, higher than it had any right to go, much to Tony's delight.

For that moment, all was well. All was idyllic. All was just as it should have been.

Then everything stopped.

The stick didn't come back down.

It spun to a jolting halt and hung there. It didn't spin, it was just impossibly still in the air, looking like a dark scar across the amber sky.

"What the hell?" Sam muttered, as he stared at the hovering stick.

Dog's barks soon came, and grew louder and more frantic, as his hackles rose, his tail jammed between his legs. He ran and cowered behind Tony's legs for safety.

The day then cut out.

Night didn't fall. Instead, it immediately snapped in. One second the sky was a beautiful, dusky hue, the next it was all black. Pure black. All the light that was given from the setting sun had blinked out to nothing, as though someone had turned off the light switch of the world. Night appeared, and with it came a strong wind, stinking of rusty metal and rancid meat. A wind that appeared as a sudden cyclone, battering around the garden. As it howled at them, it pushed Sam and Tony backward, its strength being too immense to stand against. They stumbled and staggered on their feet, desperate to keep upright.

Dog bolted, petrified, his barks now turned to whines as he raced around to the front of the house. Cowering by the closed front door.

Tony wasn't far behind him. Turning the corner from the garden, he hugged himself to the cottage wall, pushing himself against the brick. Escaping the gusts as quickly as he could.

Sam, though, had no easy escape route. He was out in the open garden, fighting against the gale. He barely had the strength to keep on his feet but slowly managed to claw his way to the back wall, where the lattice fence carried creeping ivy up from the ground.

Now the light came, but it was not the sun's return. Nor lightning. Not a car, or the moon. It was a large column. A sudden white shaft that burst from the darkness above landing in their garden. It was no normal light but a blinding whiteness that stung the eyes to look at. A light that brought with it a humming, electrical drone that joined in with the howls of the wind.

Tony, pressing himself against the wall, moved his head just far enough to glimpse his father through the storm.

Sam grabbed hold of the lattice, his teeth bared as

every muscle ached in his body. But his attempts were futile. The wind was beating into him and winning the fight, pulling him back onto the lawn, back into the light.

Something then pulled his feet off the ground. First one, then the other, as he was wrenched away, pulled up into the column of light.

"Dad!" Tony screamed, peering around the corner, but the boy's voice was weak against the cacophony.

"Tony!" Sam cried back, reaching one hand off the lattice and out to his son, but the pull was too strong.

"Dad!" the boy wailed again, but it was too late.

As Sam kept a tight grip, the lattice gave way under the force, and the ivy tore free. He was lifted, kicking against the wind as his shadow was cast down over the house, over his son, blocking out the light behind as he was yanked towards it.

One moment he was thrashing around in the wind's grip, reaching down to his son, and the next... nothing. Only emptiness remained.

The blinding glare had swallowed Sam whole.

The sun returned in a second, switched back on as if the dark had never been there. The wind also subsided into a summer breeze.

Dusk had returned, and the world righted itself in a heartbeat.

Up high, the stick was also still in the air, but it soon remembered gravity and dropped. Falling to the grass below.

Dog was still at the front door, whining. Eyes closed and body trembling.

Tony was still looking around the corner, staring in anguish at a sky that refused to explain itself.

"Dad," he whispered, as the tears fell down his face.

THREE YEARS LATER - LONDON

His sweat was sticky and cold as Tony jolted awake, gasping in terror.

His eyes were wide as reality attempted to settle in, but instead of his usual dark and quiet room, there was a shadow looming at the end of his bed, staring at him, *glaring* at him.

It was his father, Sam. Tony could tell that much, but something was different about him. Wrong.

"Dad," Tony whimpered, confused.

Sam moved his arms, lifting a Polaroid camera, not bringing it to his eyes to see through the viewfinder but just aiming it at his son.

A click and a sudden bright flash billowed from the camera and engulfed the whole room.

Tony's scream was immediately followed by the bedroom door flying open, and his mother running inside.

Rachel was in her dressing gown, carrying a look of worry, as she ran over and grabbed her son tightly.

"It's okay, baby," she said, as his scream started to

die away to sobbing. "Shhhh, shhhh, it's all okay... It was only a bad dream."

She leaned over and switched on his bedside lamp.

Tony nervously opened his eyes and looked toward the foot of the bed, then around his room. There was nothing there. No sign of his father, no trace of anything nightmarish. Just the usual clutter: stuffed toys, the half-painted model of a gunship helicopter on his desk beside his plastic toy panther, and posters of circus clowns and performing animals on the walls.

His breathing began to settle and get back to normal as Rachel wiped the tears from his cheeks.

"What was it?" she asked. "Was it Daddy again?"

Tony sadly nodded.

"What was he doing?"

"I don't know, he... had a camera," Tony shrugged, as he looked hopefully to his mother. "Is he coming home yet?"

Rachel smiled, kissing him lightly on the forehead. "How about you go back to sleep? Just lie down."

But Tony was on the verge of crying again. "What if he is stuck somewhere and can't find his way home?"

"We can talk about this in the morning, okay?" She smoothed his hair from his face, hiding her own worry from him.

Closing his door, Rachel checked her watch: 10.30 p.m. With a loud exhalation, she padded back to her bedroom.

. . .

In the darkness of the room, Joe Hayward was sleeping on the other side of their double bed. Three years her junior, he and Rachel had known each other for a long time, working as the photographer for her ad agency. But they'd been a couple for just over a year, and he had moved into her apartment after only six months.

Some people they knew gossiped that it was all too soon after Sam's disappearance, but to them, it felt like it was at the right pace. They'd fallen for each other fast and hard from the moment they allowed themselves to really see one another beyond the working relationship.

Climbing into her side of the bed, Rachel reached for her cigarette packet, pulled one out, and lit it, steadying the slight tremble in her hand.

Joe grumbled as the smell woke him. Rolling over, he flicked on the lamp. Through his bleary eyes, he could see what the issue was. He could easily tell from her worried expression.

"Tony?" he asked.

"I don't see why it's starting all over again," she said, taking a long, comforting drag. "He was doing so well, wasn't he?"

Joe rubbed her arm. "He's just getting to that age where he needs a dad. It's understandable. I mean, we're still in the same house, and it's gotta be a constant reminder of him."

With a nod, Rachel looked at him. "Maybe you should spend more time with Tony? Get to know him a bit better."

"Yeah, I would love that, you know I would," Joe replied. "But he really doesn't like me that much."

"Oh, that's not true!"

As Joe talked, he kept a comforting smile on his face. "You *know* it is. He's obsessed with his father. As he should be. Every time I try to reach out, to engage with him, it's always, '*Daddy did it this way, Daddy said that*'. And I get it. I do. 100% I understand... But to be honest, it beats me how he even remembers any of that. It was years ago, and not like Sam spent that much time with him when he was around."

"You do more for Tony than his father ever did. I had to nag all the time for Sam to pay more attention to him... It's ironic that he disappeared the *one* time he took time out of his *busy day* to play with his only son."

"Maybe, sure, but Sam was still his dad," Joe said. "And that counts for a lot... and you can't forget that his dog passed right after as well. Maybe it combined his loss. That he wishes his dad back, sure, but it's also him wanting his dog back? Ah I dunno. Kids are a mystery."

She inhaled another deep drag.

"Could he be acting out because of us?" Joe asked.

Rachel thought for a moment. "Maybe? Maybe he feels like you're replacing his dad? Ah, I don't know."

Sitting up, Joe smiled and slipped his hand inside her dressing gown. "He won't be jealous when he's got a little brother to play with." His hand slowly moved down from her belly. "We could always try to make another."

"Not quite yet," she said, pushing her worry away. "But we can always practice."

An hour earlier in the north of the country, where the mountains and plains sat ragged and wild, the storm clouds blotted out the landscape, draping it in an oily shadow.

The nearby village didn't see the shape enlarging on the horizon as it hovered across the landscape, dipping and veering across it like a floating Goliath. A vast machine that didn't even make the slightest of sounds. No combustion or mechanical noise, just the wind howling around it as it travelled on.

Looking up, it appeared as just a black mass. A nighttime shadow. That is, until the burst of light shot out from the underside. A brilliant flare that blazed, and with it came a sudden drone. Like a thousand tubas playing their lowest notes at once, it sounded like an apocalyptic herald.

The white light filled the wild field beneath it, as from the middle, the blurred outline of a form emerged from inside. An inhuman form, suspended in light, writhing as it was slowly lowered down to the ground below.

Moving lower at an incremental pace, the thing finally landed on the grass. And as its body touched the ground, the light from the machine snapped off, so did its bassy drone. This immense machine then moved off silently. Leaving the wilderness as it had found it, with the one addition.

The undergrowth surrounding the thing, for fifty feet in each direction, had been flattened. Forced down in a circular pattern by the light. And each blade of grass, each strand of weed, had been bent on its side. Forced down in submission of the extraterrestrial light.

A mist that had clung to the area now swirled as if in its own panic, carrying with it a faint, almost oily scent.

The form that came from the machine's light was left squirming on the damp leaves and weeds, enclosed in a thick, semi-transparent membrane. A gelatinous shell that coated its body from head to foot. It shimmered with a heat that didn't belong to this night. A high temperature that charred the ground beneath it.

A sudden tear in its skin and a claw broke through from inside the cocoon. Grasping, it pulled itself outward, forcing its gnarled head out. But as soon as it got out from the ruptured sack, it turned in on it and took a bite of its matter with sharp teeth. Then another. One bite after another, the slime-covered monster chewed, systematically eating the fleshy shell it had been encased within.

After a while, it had gorged on all the fleshy jelly, and the monster rose up onto its haunches. It licked away any remaining glistening mucus that clung to its skin, with a long-forked tongue. It appeared reptilian with scaled skin. Emaciated, there was no trace of any hair upon its body, and the thing's eyes sat as large red orbs, almost glowing. With its short back legs, it used its long arms to balance its walk like a gorilla.

Taking a tentative step, the thing stumbled as it adjusted to its gait. Its movements grew more assured, steadier the further it walked through the nearby woodland, toward the field on the other side.

The moon, now at its apex, broke through the gloomy clouds and lit the creature's path, all the way to a darkened cottage.

Getting to its wooden front door, the thing placed its claw upon it and pressed down hard. Within moments, the sound of the lock snapping echoed throughout the empty house as the door flung itself open.

But the thing had also left its mark on the paintwork. Where its claw had been now bubbled and smoked, in the shape of its palm and talons.

Stepping inside, the thing walked across the hallway to the small kitchen, one dominated by a large pine dining table. It walked in and unknowingly grazed the light switch, accidentally clicking it on. The bulb immediately sprang to life and soaked the room in its yellowing glow. The thing hissed as it cowered from the glare and batted the switch off again.

Despite the momentary cowering, as the darkness returned, the thing continued across to the iron stove. Despite the monster being from the skies, it knew what this was, as it grabbed the valve, switched on the gas, and leaned over the burner, taking in hungrily deep

inhalations. Greatly enjoying these escaping noxious
fumes.

2. REBIRTH

As the clock struck midnight, Kerry Digweed was in the bathtub, warm water pouring over her from the shower head. Her day had seemed endless, but at last, she could stop and let herself unwind.

Having stood there for twenty minutes, she finally pushed herself to get out. With the water turned off, she reached out blindly for the towel draped over a nearby chair, then she stepped out to dry herself off.

Putting on a silk dressing gown, she walked into her living room.

This house was small and spartan, with bare bulbs dangling in most of the cramped rooms. She was not a homely person and spent most of her days out in the fields. Farming her small plot of land was her life and her passion.

Her small terrier, Clive, was waiting by the door. Pacing back and forth, he was anxiously whining to Kerry.

"What's the matter?" she asked, walking across to a nearby window. "Someone out there?"

The dog whined again.

All that Kerry could see out was the night. Even her garden was invisible through the darkness.

With a shrug, she turned and walked back to the kitchen.

"Come on, 'fraidy cat," she laughed. "Let's get you some food."

As soon as Clive heard that word, his composure changed. The whine was replaced by a lolling tongue as he hopped on all fours, merrily to the kitchen.

Kerry laughed, watching him bound ahead in front of her.

In the tiny kitchen, her dishes and cutlery sat in piles on the counter, as on the stove, a pot of stew sat cooling from her earlier meal.

"Should be cold enough now," she said, grabbing Clive's bowl from the floor.

She ladled in some of the stew, all whilst he happily hopped in place.

"Here you go, you silly thing."

As she bent down to give him his dish, she didn't see the shape that lurked at the window, its bulbous eyes reflecting the kitchen light upon their shiny surface. The dog didn't sense anything either, as it focused solely on the food it now ate.

A few moments later, a single rap dragged both of their attention to the front door.

Kerry looked down at Clive, who was on high alert again. The lure of his food only temporary.

Cautiously, she walked back into the living room and flicked on the porch light, then opened the door.

"Hello?" she asked to no one there. But she did catch a caustic whiff of burning. Stepping back, she noticed that a patch of the door that was bubbling and blistering from where something had touched it.

Clive soon began barking as he stood in the middle of the room, looking out past her.

"Shh!" Kerry said as she stepped back in and slammed the door. "Quiet, boy. It's too late for that racket."

She looked back and peeked out of the curtains again, her hackles as raised as Clive's, just without the noise. She could sense something was wrong, but she couldn't see what. She shut the curtains tight to block out whatever was out there.

To make sure, she walked back into the kitchen, reached for the lock on the back door, and bolted it shut. Feeling an immediate relief, she pulled the curtains closed over that window too.

Clive had followed her back in, glanced at the food left in his bowl, but was too anxious about what he sensed to finish. He then looked around unsure.

"I don't like this either boy," she whispered. "We're probably both being stupid.... right?"

Then a loud slam of a window upstairs startled her, also making Clive whelp and cower under the table.

"It's okay, Clive, it's just upstairs. Nothing's climbing in up there," she said to the petrified dog as well as her own fear. "But I'll get the gun, and check anyway, that sound good with you?" She then shook her head. "It's just the fucking wind, what's wrong with me?"

Still, she went to the large cupboard to retrieve her double-barrelled shotgun.

As she grabbed its handle, she felt a sticky sheen on it and felt a sudden pang of fear. She had no time to think, though, as the door crashed open. The reptilian visitor erupted. Its movement impossibly fast, as it shot out in blur of scales and fabric, its broken bone clacking loudly with each move.

She tried to scream as its broken hands clamped around her arms and lifted her up like she weighed nothing.

The screams bellowed from her chest as it carried her into the middle of the room, to the table where Clive hid, and slammed her down upon it. The wood made a splintering crack as the thing quickly straddled her, pressing her down with a weight that pinned every motion.

The thing had to hurry, as it had little time. It could feel its body getting weaker.

She screamed more, struggling to fight away this unstoppable force. She stared at its exposed face. The slick scaled thing looming over her: its large eyes like wet glass, and rows of serrated teeth glinting down at her.

But it was not this monster grip on her that caused

her the most terror; it was what was coming out from its mouth: several tentacle-like proboscides that extended out of its throat, trailing down toward Kerry's mouth.

These protrusions glistened as they fluttered toward her, brushing her skin with curiosity along the way, tasting her.

She twisted, pushed, and kicked, but the thing's strength was too great. As its appendages coiled closer, Clive shuddered under the table, too petrified to attack or protect.

Then finally, her screams became strangled as the tentacles reached her mouth and jammed inside as one. Burying deep down her throat and into her body.

Kerry was still on the table in her living room when she started to wake. The memory of her attack was now a haze that seemed almost like a nightmare.

The lights in the house were switched off, and the room around her was barely lit by the night sky shining in through the now opened front door.

Each part of her body felt battered as she slid off the table and got to her feet. She exhaled painfully as she straightened her back and took a step toward the door.

Her spit felt thick, like she had swallowed glue, sitting almost gelatinous in her mouth as she gasped to keep breathing.

With each step she took, she started to remember.

The noises.

The wardrobe.

That *thing*...

Staggering, Kerry peered out into the night, where she saw her dog, gnawing on something large that lay in the long grass.

"Clive?" she said. But her voice was strangled and weak.

The dog, though hearing her, paid little attention to her call, and continued gnawing.

Kerry stepped outside, not feeling the cold concrete of the porch beneath her feet. "Clive? Boy?" She called out again.

The dog, sensing her nearby, tore a piece from what it was eating and scampered into the dark. But as it went, Kerry could see what it carried. She could clearly make out the outline of a claw. Clive was carrying the hand of the thing that had attacked her.

Her shocked gaze then fell to the mass on the lawn: They were the rest of its remains. The beast's body had rapidly deteriorated and was now barely recognisable as a life form. There was what looked like an eye, maybe? Were those its legs? The stolen hand seemed to be all that was left of the creature that was now dissolving into the dirt beneath it.

Seeing the grotesquerie, Kerry felt her stomach lurch. She ran back into the house, into the bathroom and retched into the sink, releasing all the half-digested stew from the evening. But not only that, along with the vomit came lumps of congealed blood.

Panicking as she saw it, she turned on the tap, thrust her mouth underneath the cold flow, and gulped to get rid of the vile taste of copper and bile.

Looking up, the small bathroom mirror reflected her tearful anguish.

With her head falling into her hands, she sat down heavily onto the rim of the bathtub.

"What the fuck's happening to me?" she wept.

Before she could think, a sudden slice of pain ripped through her belly. Causing her to bend over in agony. A growing throb that now pushed her belly suddenly outward, inflating like a balloon.

"Help," she wailed in desperation as she clambered into the living room, trying to get to her telephone. But she only managed three steps when her knees buckled, sending her collapsing to the wood.

Crying out, she turned onto her back and gripped her stomach, which was now swelling impossibly large. Her flesh now made a squeaking, tearing sound as her abdomen was pushed to its limit.

Her memory then opened as she remembered the tentacle-like things that choked her. Went deep into her. The face of the monster above her.

From between her legs, a gush of dark blood erupted, spraying out onto her dressing gown. She didn't notice this happening as her body had started to convulse violently, and her screaming became a constant.

Pain radiated from her stomach and down into her groin as the swelling went beyond any form of pregnancy. Her stomach bloated and bloated, until her muscle and skin with an audible rip and her internal organs began to rupture. The blood that pooled from her began to spurt out lumps of intestine and bowel.

The torment she was going through was so intense that her screams faded, leaving her silently trying to make a noise, but all that could be heard was her own body being torn from the inside.

Her back arched as her legs spread. Her hip bones snapped in two as her vagina started to open, something inside her was pushing its way out into the world.

From within, a hairy mass pushed its way out. And as it moved, it ripped apart the inside of her torso. Heart and lungs immediately pulverised as the thing lunged up, ripping through her stomach tissue.

As it got up, it grew taller until it stood over six feet tall. Not a monster, but a man.

Covered in the blood, shit and gory remnants of Kerry Digweed, this naked figure stretched his new body. He then looked down and saw that from his stomach, an umbilical cord wound down between him and the corpse of his unwilling mother.

He grabbed it in one hand and bit down, tearing himself free from the fleshy tether.

In the dark, this man then noticed a mess of afterbirth. He would soon consume that too.

3. MOTHER'S MILK

Under a stretch of leaning trees, beneath their leafless canopy, a Volkswagen Beetle drove slowly along the winding country road.

Ben Minkle had just turned thirty and had spent the last five hours in the car with his girlfriend, Jane Baker. With a road atlas on her lap and a flashlight in her hand she was studying the page with a confused expression.

"Which road did you say we were on?" she asked, trying to make sense of the squiggles on the page.

"Haversham Road, I think?" He sighed, looking around at the lack of any signs of life. But there were no houses, no shops, just trees and fields.

"I... I can't find that," she said. "It's just not on here... I told you we should haven't taken the back road."

"Great way to spend my birthday." he moaned, as

he squinted through the windscreen, trying to see the road through Jane's flashlight glare. "Can you turn that out?" he asked. "Can't see a thing here... Besides, we don't wanna wake her, do we? Can't do with being lost and her screaming for our attention."

Jane switched the flashlight off and looked to the back seat. There, a cot sat, where inside, their one-month-old was fast asleep. Twitching softly in her dreams.

"She's fine," Jane said with a smile. "She'll probably need a feeding soon." She turned back to face the front. And as she did, the car's headlight caught the skin of a naked man walking directly in front of them across the road,

"LOOK OUT!" Jane screamed, as she put one hand back to brace the cot.

Ben tried to swerve, tried to avoid the figure, but it all happened too quick.

The bumper slammed into the figure with a loud thump, sending it down under the car's wheels, jolting the car up violently.

Tony was in bed, in a fitful sleep. The nightmares were flooding his unconsciousness once more. He cried out, as his face winced in pain, his dreams breaking through to reality.

. . .

The brakes slammed on, screeching the tyres along the asphalt as Ben yanked the wheel. The car swerved, running off the road and into the tree line.

Tony's back arched as his nightmare contorted his body. His whole frame lost all control as it lurched, sending him off the bed in a mass of tangled, urine-drenched sheets.

With the Volkswagen now stopped in a mass of branches, Ben turned in a panic. The baby was okay but crying in shock, Jane reaching to settle her.

"It's okay baby," she said, trying to stay calm. "Shhhh... Shhhh."

Throwing the door open, Ben got out and ran onto the road, out through the darkness towards the scene of the collision.

Hearing Jane open her passenger door behind him, he turned and called back. "Stay in the car!"

But she didn't listen. With her daughter falling back to sleep, having forgotten the loud noise that only just woke her, Jane was now outside the car, assessing the car's damage.

Moving gingerly around the front, she shone the flashlight on the crumpled bumper, putting her hand out to touch it. There was a glaze on its chrome. Like a thick honey. A sticky covering that made her feel sick as she touched it.

"Ew, gross," she said with a grimace, wiping her hand on her jeans.

Tony woke up as he fell out of bed, hitting the bedroom floor.

"Mummy," he moaned, feeling the pain wracking his body.

He slowly staggered to his feet and made his way into the hallway.

"Mummy," he whimpered again.

He was too agony-riddled to scream as he hobbled down towards his mother's bedroom. Every part of him felt in pain. From head to his toes, each bone and muscle stung like it had been pummelled.

Getting to the bedroom door, hunched over, he pushed it open with one hand, as the other gripping his ribs.

There on the bed was his mother, bent over as Joe was behind her, thrusting hard. Their naked bodies sweating in ecstasy.

Their smiles of pleasure soon fell away as they noticed Tony in the doorway—staring at them in horror as he collapsed to the carpet.

With a worried yelp, Rachel scrambled off the bed to her unconscious son.

Ben was still on the road, wishing he had brought the

flashlight as he looked for what he hit. But the road was empty.

"What the hell?" he mumbled to himself, before calling back. "There's no one here."

He turned his gaze to the shallow banks and ditches on either side. But before he could convince himself that he hit an animal that had now scampered away, a rustling came from the nearby bushes.

Rushing over to investigate, Ben climbed up on the bank and peeked over a thorny brush to where he saw the naked figure of a man kneeling in the dirt. He appeared to be bent forward, his side covered in blood. His spine had broken through his skin, and his neck was cracked at a terrifying angle.

"S-shit," Ben stammered. "Are you okay? I'll get help."

He reached out. His fingers brushing against the man's ice-cold skin.

The instant he touched, the man's spine arched and straightened with a sharp crack, with bones snapping back into place.

His head then clicked upright as he turned.

Ben was too petrified to do anything. He wanted to run, but before he could, the man let out a terrifying high-pitched noise.

His mouth opened, and from within a long forked tongue shot out like a dart. Sharp and strong, it extended two feet, straight into Ben's eye socket, piercing through the bone and grey matter, until it touched the inside of his skull. It then pulled back out, bringing a chunk of brain along with it.

Ben was left, bleeding heavily from his mouth and empty eye. Trying to breathe, but his throat and whole body were short-circuiting, unable to function from the brutal damage to his mind. His comprehension and understanding were a mess as he collapsed on to the bank. Dead in a slumped heap.

Jane was back in the car, looking out of the open window, thinking she heard something.

"Ben?" she called out. "If you can't find anything, let's just go. The car looks fine to drive."

Unaware of her husband's demise, she switched off the car's interior light and flicked on her flashlight. Leaning out of the window, she shone the beam across the road but saw nothing.

"Ben?" she called out again.

The baby stirred but didn't wake at the noise.

Jane slid herself over the gearstick and into the driver's seat. Starting the engine, she shifted the Volkswagen into reverse. The car rumbled off the embankment, over the already crushed bushes, until it rolled onto the road—narrowly missing a steel drum that sat at the edge of the verge.

Glancing out the window, she breathed a sigh of relief that she hadn't slammed into it.

Quickly killing the engine, she picked her flashlight up once more and got out of the car. She looked at the steel drum as she walked up and peered inside. Lying at the bottom was a mound of broken glass. She wondered why such a thing was here until she saw the small pile of old window frames stacked nearby, their paint long since flaked off, their glass missing. An obvious dumping ground for some lazy builder.

She turned back to the road, ignoring the fly tipping, and walked on. She stepped slowly, her heels clacking on the solid ground as she moved the flashlight left and right, covering every part of the darkness ahead.

The beam soon caught on a patch of red and white. To a man's shoe that lay on its side by the side of the road. It was Ben's white leather shoe, now murky with a dripping redness across it.

Scared and barely able to even whisper his name, she hurried back to the car. She couldn't think straight as she got back behind the wheel, locked the doors, and rolled up the windows.

She risked another glance behind her, hoping to see Ben laughing, having just played a stupid prank. But there was nothing. Only the night.

Then came a loud thump above them, startling the baby awake with a scream that matched the Jane's own.

A gloopy red trail started to slide down the windscreen, slow at first, then thickening as it spread across the glass, drenching her view completely.

Another heavy impact, as something wet and solid hit the glass with a crack. The glass immediately webbed among the blood.

Jane couldn't see it, but it was Ben. Stripped of

clothing, with his head hanging over the roof's edge, having been flung onto the car.

She spun around, screaming uncontrollably along with her baby, as the fear consumed them both.

Then, there was a sudden knock on the driver's window.

Jane was ready to scream again but instead saw the familiar jacket and shirt. *Ben's* jacket and shirt.

Upon recognising it, she opened the door, ready to yell at him for whatever trick this was that he was playing. But what was stood there was not him. It was the man now dressed in his clothes. Wearing his shirt that had been covered in blood.

He lunged at her, gripping her face with his large hand. Then in an instant, snapped her neck with terrifying ease. She didn't have time to make a sound, only the gurgle from her throat as her life ended.

The man then pushed her still twitching body over to the passenger seat and climbed into the driver's side.

He then turned to her, lifting one finger and prodded her now vacant head. It lolled lifelessly, as he examined the results of his handiwork. But as it did, the man caught a scent of something. Something that made a purr escape his lips.

With one hand, he reached for her blouse and clawed it open. Her naked breasts sagged out, engorged with milk.

Unable to stop himself, he leaned forward and hungrily attached to one breast, biting down hard enough for his teeth to slice through the skin,

As he suckled hard and noisily, a mixture of mother's milk and blood filled his gullet.

Tony was in his bed, still whimpering in pain. His gaze was fixed onto the ceiling above, wide and lost. His skin now deathly and pale.

Rachel was sitting on the bed next to him, back in her dressing gown. She put one hand on his forehead to check his temperature. "Shall we get you something to drink? A hot drink maybe?"

"Hurts," was all Tony could muster.

"You'll be fine," she reassured, before turning to Joe, who was by the door. The look she gave him had no smile and instead was uncertain and scared.

Back to Tony her forced smile returned.

"Is it your arm?" she asked.

He whimpered again as a fresh wave of agony hit his nerves. He crumbled up, gripping his stomach.

She pulled back the sheets to see what he was clutching.

"Oh my God!" she cried, as she looked down. He and the sheets around him were totally saturated in blood.

"Oh my God!" she repeated as she reached and unbuttoned his pyjamas.

She let out a scream when she saw what was underneath, a blackened area covering the boy's left side and arm.

"What the fuck!?" Joe said, as he moved closer,

wide-eyed at the blood and bruising. "When the hell did he do that?"

Rachel could barely reply. "It's... black... so black..."

Joe leaned beside her and pulled Tony's pyjamas aside more, trying to look for a wound, a source of the pooling blood, but couldn't find a thing. Rachel was now holding her mouth in shock, staring at Tony's frail, battered body.

He whimpered again in pain, which sent Rachel into more hysterics.

All the noise had woken the twenty-year-old French girl in the next bedroom. Analise, Tony's au pair.

She wiped her eyes as she looked in from the doorway.

"What is the matter?" she said in a thick Parisian accent.

"Somebody call the doctor!" Rachel screamed.

Joe quickly stood and rushed over to the au pair. "Get some towels, linen... anything... Okay?"

Shaken by the urgency, Analise nodded and rushed down the hallway, as Joe ran downstairs to the kitchen.

Rachel was quickly removing the rest of Tony's bloody clothes as she stared all over his body for any bloody gash or gouge.

Joe could be heard on the phone, shouting for the doctor. Saying he didn't care what time it was, that it was an emergency.

Analise rushed in carrying a few white towels, which she handed to Rachel as he was hit with the shock of seeing Tony covered in red.

Rachel cried as she took a towel and wiped the blood off his body.

In the Volkswagen, the sounds of slurping and chewing had stopped. The man sat up from his feeding, feeling satiated and full.

Jane's body stared emptily, as both of her breasts had been torn away from her chest, the milk and flesh both consumed, leaving only bloody holes.

The tip of his forked tongue darted over his milky chin, lapping up the final drops that had dripped down.

As he had fed on her, the man had heard the baby crying but had paid it no attention. Not until now. Now the noise it made had become piercing. Almost agony in the man's head.

Reaching back, with one hand he picked up the baby by her head, and held her in front of him, dangling as he assessed it.

Not enough meat for a meal.

Not of any sizeable threat.

Of no possible use.

The driver's side door opened, and the man got out, as the screaming infant dangled from its grip, her shawl sliding to the tarmac.

Pulling Ben's naked body off the roof with his free

hand, the man then turned and dropped the baby casually into the steel drum on the verge. Discarding it straight into the long, sharp shards of glass that lay inside.

The wailing ceased instantly, leaving only silence.

"No pain at all?" Doctor Scott asked as he prodded the boy's side.

Still in his bed, now wearing a fresh pair of pyjamas on changed bedding, Tony's skin was back to its usual colour, the bruising on his torso now completely gone, and his cheeks were no longer pale and flushed pink. The only evidence of something untoward was the pile of bloody towels and sheets that were lumped beside the bed.

Behind the doctor, Rachel and Joe stood there with a mutually pensive and worried look.

"I'm okay," Tony replied with a happy smile.

Analise quietly walked in and grabbed the bloody pile by the bed.

"Thank you," Joe said quietly as she walked out. "Just put them in the machine, and we'll wash them in the morning."

The Doctor closed Tony's pyjama shirt. "Alright then, folks," he said with a smile. "We should let this little soldier get back to sleep."

Standing, he picked up his doctor's bag. Rachel moved by to give Tony a kiss goodnight.

"Doctor?" Joe said, following the doctor into the

hallway. "I thought it was internal bleeding, but I couldn't find a wound. Then it just... went, just like that. It's weird right?"

"Please can you tell me what time it is, Mr. Phillips?" the Doctor asked, sternly.

"Uhh, I'm not actually Mr. Phillips, but..." Joe quickly looked at his watch. "... It's 4.30."

Rachel walked out of the bedroom, quietly closing the door behind her.

"Yes. 4.30 *a.m.*" the doctor replied with a grunt. "No, there was no wound, and certainly there was never any bleeding, internally nor externally."

Rachel looked at him in confusion. "But there was so much blood! You saw it on the towels, and on the bedsheets."

With a tired sigh, Doctor Scott tried his best to not lose his temper. "May I ask, has he played this kind of trick before?"

"Trick?" Joe said. "What do you mean?"

"That was some sort of animal blood," he replied. "I could tell that as soon as I walked in. The pungency. It's unmistakable. My guess would be pig, or goat. But I can tell you categorically that it was not your son's, nor was it even human."

"That's impossible," Rachel said, looking to Joe for some reassurance.

"Mrs. Phillips," he added. "There is nothing whatsoever wrong with your son. He has a healthy complexion. Not a mark or even a blemish on his body. His temperature is quite normal. If you want my professional opinion from over forty years of general practice, then he has an overworked imagination that's crying out for your attention. Now, please, it is far too late for this utter nonsense. Your son should be told off, and I should be back in bed."

4. CHANGE

Breakfast for Rachel was usually a happy time, where she, Tony, and Joe would sit down and happily eat whilst discussing what they had planned for the day. But this morning was different. Rachel hadn't managed any more sleep since the doctor left—unlike Joe, who went straight to sleep and snored loudly.

Tony, though, was just as excitable as he usually was at this time and now enthusiastically finished off his bacon and eggs.

Rachel stood at the stove, zoning out of the cooking as she stared blankly at the wall.

"Can I have another egg?" Tony asked.

But she didn't hear him.

"Mummy?"

Snapped from her distraction, Rachel turned with a forced smile.

"Hmm?" she said.

"Egg? Can I have another egg?" he repeated.

"How about you say please?"

He rolled his eyes. "Fine. Pleaaaaaase?"

Rachel motioned to his plate "Finish what you have first, okay?"

Tony nodded as he went back to eating. "Can I have some orange as well?" he asked with a mouthful of bacon.

Walking over to the refrigerator, she took out the carton of orange juice and poured him a glass.

Sitting opposite at the table, she watched as he ate and played with his toy soldier between mouthfuls. A small plastic commando figure, that he made walk across the table, climb over the ketchup bottle, around the butter tray, all while he mimed shooting various items—complete with food filled sound effects.

"Look, Mummy," he said, as he made his toy scale the cardboard cereal box and drop inside, along with a small scream. Tony found it all extremely funny and shrieked with delight.

"Yes, dear, that's marvellous," she said, trying to stay awake. "Now come on and finish your breakfast if you want that egg."

Shovelling in the last mouthfuls at once, he looked at her with a packed grin. "Can I have it now, please?" he said in a muffle.

She smiled and got up, shovelling an egg from the pan onto his plate.

She then turned to the open door and called out. "Analise?"

No answer.

"Analise?" After a moment she tutted.

"Joe?" Rachel's voice carried through the house.

Stood on the landing, Joe leaned over the banister.

"What is it?" he called back.

"Check Analise is up, will you?" came her reply.

With a shrug, Joe turned around and walked over to the au pair's bedroom door, knocking on it loudly.

"Hey, Analise?" he said loudly. "You up?"

He knocked again.

With no reply, he gingerly opened the door and looked inside the dark room. The sunlight was unable to break past the thick curtains that hung across the window.

"Come on, Analise," he sighed, walking over to the curtains and opening them wide. "Tony time!"

Joe walked into the kitchen shaking his head.

"I'm telling you; she could sleep through a bomb dropping."

"Is she up?" Rachel asked.

"Who knows? I tried." Joe smiled, walking over to the kettle to pour himself a coffee.

Rachel was not amused. She was too tired to find anything funny.

"Joe," she said sadly. "Please."

"She always looks half asleep to me anyway, so I

can't really tell." He sat at the table with his coffee. "She moves so slow I don't even think blood moves around her body." He smiled Tony, who was fishing in the cereal box to get his commando figure back.

"Hey," Joe said before turning to Rachel, mouthing the words *'Is he okay?'*

"Hello, Joe," Tony replied, paying more attention to his toy.

"What are we all doing today then?" Joe asked. Trying to install some normality onto the morning.

Rachel smiled at his effort. "You gotta re-shoot the pack on that beer commercial for a start."

"Again?" Joe's shoulders slumped before turning to Tony. "Oh, I forgot to say, I'm photographing some cool old planes on Monday. Even got a couple of Spitfires there. You wanna come along, and see?"

"No," Tony replied, making his commando jump off his empty plate onto the table.

"No? Why not?" Joe said dejectedly. "You like planes, don't you?"

"They're boring," came the boy's response.

As he spoke, the collar of Tony's shirt lifted, and from underneath the head of a small, thin snake appeared, slithering out.

"Tony, come on!" Rachel scolded. "I told you I won't have Harry in the kitchen. Take him out, now! Put him back upstairs."

With a sigh, Tony got out of his seat and helped the snake come out of his shirt to wrap around his hand.

"Come on, boy," he said quietly to his small pet. "Let's put you back in your bed."

Without another word, the boy and snake left the kitchen and went back upstairs.

"That boy really needs a firm hand." Joe said, jokingly mimed a spanking action to Rachel. "Bam!" he said. But when he saw Rachel's maudlin expression, his joke dropped. "What did he have to say about last night?"

"He doesn't remember anything, apparently."

"That's just rubbish, you're not going to let him get away with it, are you? You heard the doctor."

Rachel stifled a yawn. "I believe him."

"How? Nothing seems wrong with him today." He motioned to Tony's empty breakfast plate. "And his appetite is fine."

"I don't know... I just know what we saw. He couldn't have faked it... And even if he could, where the hell did he get all that blood from?"

Joe didn't want to fight, but he didn't agree. "Whatever, he just saw us at it. He saw more of both of us than he should. Me in particular. Could have made him do anything."

"In the twenty minutes between him collapsing and being put into bed, he just... what? Decided to do that?"

At a petrol station along a country road, an old Ford

registered to one Kerry Digweed pulled up into the small forecourt.

In the station's small shop, the attendant—a lanky, sour-looking man in his fifties—looked up wearily from his book, watching this car stop by one of the pumps. He raised an eyebrow as a man got out of the car.

The man seemed fine, but wore a jacket over the bloody shirt, and wore no shoes on his feet.

"Another bloody nutter," the attendant moaned, as he reached forward and called out of the window. "Fill it up?"

The man turned and nodded to him.

Without any thought the man's gaze fell to the window of the car door. To his reflection. To his reborn reflection.

There he was.

Sam Phillips.

Same hair, same face, same body, same memories as the day he was lifted off the ground. But the memories were not his. Not really.

His remembered the family that had been left behind, and he felt... *something*. He felt clearer. Like he was waking up from a dream.

Noticing a payphone on the wall, Sam walked over, rummaged in his pockets, until he pulled out a small clutch of coins.

Throwing in 10p, he lifted the receiver and dialled. A number he had remembered.

· · ·

From the kitchen, the telephone rang loudly as Rachel put on her coat in the other room.

"One moment," she shouted, as she rushed in, fumbling her arm through the coat's woollen sleeve.

"Hello?" She said, picking up the phone with her free hand.

Instead of a voice, there was a sea of static. Clicking and buzzing in her ear.

"Hello?" she repeated.

Through the noise came a word. A faint whisper repeated: *Rachel. Rachel. Rachel. Rachel.*

Over and over, it said that through the electric hum, but it was so weak that no age or sex could be assigned to the voice. It was just a heard word.

"Hello?" She said, finding the static quite painful to listen to. "Sorry, I can't hear you, it's an awful line."

For a beat, the noise subsided, as the voice came through clearer. A male voice. A voice that almost hissed her name...

"Rachel."

With shock, she put down the receiver and stared at the phone, feeling a chill. Knowing that voice.

At the petrol station, Sam stood with his mouth open. Unable to speak, aside from repeating her name in a whisper.

In his hand, smoke began to rise from the phone, now beeping with a call-ended tone. The plastic he held was melting and buckling in his hands. The electrics inside now buzzing and short-circuiting.

Letting it drop from his grip, the plastic fell uselessly to the floor, breaking free from its cable tether.

His mind then began to fog again, as he felt himself falling into the dark.

"Rachel," he whispered.

The attendant, meanwhile, had left the confines of his shop and walked over to the car, ready to fill it up.

Sam shook off the momentary lapse, as he walked to the door marked *Toilets*.

In the dank, piss smelling room, there was one cubicle, a browning urinal and a cracked sink. Sam walked straight over to the mirror and looked at himself through the grime that was caked to its surface.

The memories he carried were like a weight he had to fight to control.

He didn't know how long he had spent staring at himself, repeating his wife's name under his breath but when he turned to the window, he noticed the attendant. The lanky man looked annoyed, having filled the car's tank with petrol and now stood waiting for his return.

Sam turned back to the sink, ran the tap, and washed the slightly murky water over his face.

. . .

The attendant was getting impatient.

"What are you doing in there?" he mumbled staring at the toilet door. "Ten bloody minutes?"

Striding over from the pumps, he didn't want to wait any longer.

Pushing the toilet door open, he didn't look in as he spoke.

"That's your petrol done," he called in.

No response came, so he looked inside.

There was no one by the sink, and the cubicle door was closed.

"Hey mate," he added. "Need some oil? Tyres pumped up?"

Still no reply.

"What are you doing in here?" the attendant asked, annoyed. "You okay?"

Having had enough, the attendant pushed on the cubical door.

It swung inward with ease.

Sam was there, standing in front of the toilet. Just staring back.

"That's it, give me the money and get out."

Not answering, Sam looked at his own bloodied clothes, then at the attendants.

He then stepped forward, grabbed the man's belt, and began to unbuckle it.

"Hey, I don't want no funny business," was all the attendant managed to say as Sam pulled his belt out, then gripped the man by the neck. Lifting him off the ground without any effort, out of the cubicle, and across the bathroom.

Slamming him to the floor, the attendant yelped. His back spasming in sharp pain.

"There's no money," he gasped. "Christ, you're my first customer.... Please."

But Sam was not listening and busily unbuttoned the overalls, pulling them off him, whilst still pinning him to the floor by a firm grip in his neck.

"No, no, no, no," the man wheezed as he thrashed to stop his clothes being removed. "Please... no!"

Sam shot a glare at so ferocious that it made the man stop kicking out in fear.

His clothes were quickly removed and thrown to the corner of the bathroom, as Sam's grip on his neck remained firm. His eyes then moved to the attendant's chest.

Though what the attendant dreaded didn't come to pass... something *much* worse did.

Sam's mouth opened, and the collection of glistening, black proboscides emerged.

As the attendant tried to scream, the grip around his windpipe tightened, throttling any sound from coming out.

The tentacle-like tendrils fell onto the man's bare chest and pierced the skin on impact, which caused his body to buck, but it was futile.

Each proboscis dug into the skin and trailed visibly under the skin, traversing over his ribcage, forming an elaborate network of welts across the man's chest.

The attendant soon lost consciousness as the pain got too much.

Then the real brutality began, as Sam started to move his mouth closer, and his tendrils worked their way beneath the ribs and around the man's internal organs.

Sam needed to feed. He was only just reborn after all.

5. HOMECOMING

Tony was dressed in his school uniform of brown shorts, white shirt and brown tie as he stood on his bed. Holding his toy helicopter in his hand, he whooshed it around, playing pretend as if it were in a battle with an invisible enemy.

He made the sound of enemy gunfire that hit into the toy's propeller, sending it careening down to the floor. He dropped the toy off the side of the bed, making the noise of a loud explosion as it clacked to the carpet.

"Allez, allez, you little horror," Analise called cheerily from the doorway. "Time for school. Let's go, let's go, let's go!"

By dawn, the stolen Ford had already made it to the city. And the journey felt like a half-remembered dream. The streets and roads each flickered across

Sam's memory. All the images belonged to him, but not to the thing inside.

He had left the car on a side street and carried on foot. Now dressed in the mechanic's overalls, he moved through the morning crowd unseen, hearing names and fragments of language that meant nothing yet everything. Somewhere, beneath the human buzz, something else lurked. Recollection that called to him. A pulse that tugged inside, and he followed it.

The pulse grew stronger when he got to a street that he knew all too well.

Walking down the stone staircase of the apartment building, Analise and Tony reached the next floor down.

"Hello," came an old woman's voice.

Mrs. Goodman lived below. In her seventies and dressed in a massive towelling dressing gown, she always made it a point to be at her door to say goodbye to Tony on his way to school. Mainly to interject herself into other people's lives.

"How's my little pineapple this morning?" she asked, stepping onto the landing.

"Hello!" Tony replied as he reluctantly walked over and gave her a hug, something he knew he had to do and didn't like one bit.

"Bonjour, Madame Goodman," Analise said with a smile. Wishing for one morning they could get out without this happening.

"Bonjour," the old lady replied in her best French accent, before ruffling Tony's hair. "Young man, you're looking so lovely this morning I could just gobble you up!" Pinching his cheek, she shooed him away with her hand. "No go on, go enjoy yourself at school. And same to you, mademoiselle!"

And with that, Mrs. Goodman went back inside her apartment.

Tony grumbled as he continued down the stairs.

"I hate her, she smells."

Analise had to hide her laugh, as she looked back to make sure the old woman had gone. "She's nice, she likes you, Tony."

"You know, if we took the lift, we wouldn't have to see her!" he said, pointing to the small shaft that ran down the middle of the stairwell.

"Bah, I don't like that thing," she replied. "Stairs are much nicer."

As she put her raincoat on, Tony marched ahead down the remaining flight to the lobby, walking over to the glass door and onto the street.

"Wait for me," Analise called out, hurrying up after him.

The walk to school was always the same. They walked down the busy city street, through the throng of morning traffic. Navigating small side streets for twenty minutes until they arrived at the playground in front of his school.

This morning was slightly different though, not that they would know it.

As they came out of the apartment, someone was watching from the other side of the street. Sam.

Getting to the playground, the school bell rang.

"We made it!" Tony shouted.

"Only just!" Analise added.

Around them, the last stragglers of students ran to their classrooms.

She bent down and hugged Tony with a kiss on his cheek.

"I hope I don't smell like Madame Goodman," she laughed.

Neither of them noticed Sam, who had followed them here, and now stared through the railings.

Having left Tony to his day, Analise didn't go straight home. Instead, she ventured along a nearby stretch of high-end shops. Ones that were designer outlets and jewellers, selling items far beyond her means. She was not here to shop, though, she was waiting for someone.

Looking in at a Versace window display, she smiled, not at the handbags, but at the reflection of the man who approached from behind. Wrapping his arms around her waist and pushing himself against her.

"Your money or your life," he said in a gruff voice.

She turned with a giggle and wrapped her arms around his shoulders.

It was Michael Nolan. A decade older than her, he was a smooth charmer of a man, dressed in a pinstripe suit, and totally besotted with her.

From down the street, from the shadows of a closed shop's doorway, a pair of extraterrestrial eyes watched them intently.

"Taxi?" Michael asked with a cheeky grin.

"You English men, you can never wait," Analise teased.

Rachel stood at the side of the studio watching Joe setting up the needed shot.

Behind a brightly lit plinth, Joe's assistant moved a silver reflector, bouncing the brightness from the lights back onto the subject; a glass of beer.

Joe watched through the viewfinder of his camera.

"Stan, I can still see it," he said. "Move a bit more to the left a bit..."

Stan moved the reflector.

"...A bit more..."

He moved it again.

"A *smidge* more..."

The reflector was moved even further.

"Perfect! Mark that."

Through the lens, the light illuminated the bubbles of the beer even brighter.

Stan hurriedly attached a stand to the reflector, and stepped away, as the phone rang in the office at the back. He hurried to answer it.

"Rachel, where's the model gone?" Joe asked, still looking at the beer through the camera.

"Toilet, again," she answered shaking her head.

Stan came rushing back. "Rachel? I think it's for you," he said.

"Who is it?" she asked.

"Beats me," Stan shrugged. "Couldn't hear a thing, just your name."

"Fuck me, not another one," she said.

"Another what?" Joe asked.

But she had already crossed to the back of the studio and picked up the receiver, fully intending to shout at whoever it was who was prank calling her.

"Hello?" she said sternly.

"Who is it?" Joe called out from the studio.

Relieved, Rachel smiled. "It's okay, it's just Analise!"

Michael Nolan's studio flat was a chaotic example of a bachelor pad. There was the latest tech, gadget, a big television, but little organisation, and no care for mess. His clothes from the past week were either bunched on the chairs or all over the floor. Dirty plates lay in the sink, waiting for someone else, *anyone* else, to clean them.

Michael had his mouth full.

Both were naked on the bed, his face buried between Analise's legs, with his tongue working overtime as she tried to talk on the telephone.

"No, just girls from my English class," she said, biting her lip, as she tried to ignore the waves of pleasure. "Yes, but if I go it means you would have to pick up Tony... is that alright?"

As Rachel answered on the line, Michael's fingers slipped in. Analise tensed up as she fought to suppress a moan.

"Are you sure?" she said.

As Michael moved his fingers in and out, Analise tightened her thighs to tell him to stop. Which he did, but for only a few seconds.

"Thank you so much, I just thought it would be a pity to turn down the offer... Yes, yes."

He stopped obeying her and slid them in once more.

She gritted her teeth, though tried her best to cover for it.

"You too... Yes, it's a terrible line... One moment..." she reached down and smacked Michael on the top of his head. He stopped what he was doing again and looked at her apologetically. She mouthed the word 'Stop'.

She spoke back into the phone. "Hello? Sorry... Yes, of course... Okay, you too, goodbye."

. . .

As the bell sounded the end of the school day, the children came out of the building and rushed onto the playground. Some ran for the minibus waiting at the curb, others met their waiting parents or guardians.

Today though was the first time that Rachel was stood waiting for this long. Usually Tony was one of the first out the door, eager to get home. But today, Rachel had been a few minutes late and now stood watching over two hundred children leave. She had seen the minibus drive off, full of excitable cheers, and had seen every other adult meet their child and leave hand in hand.

Soon, it was just her, alone on the playground as the last child had gone.

Before she could make her way inside the school to ask where her son was, a young teacher walked over with a smile.

"Mrs. Phillips?" she asked.

Rachel looked blankly, totally forgetting this teacher's name, only remembering that she was the form tutor for Tony's year.

"Is he inside?" Rachel asked.

"Oh, there must be a mix-up of timetables," the teacher laughed. "Mr. Phillips picked him up just after the bell rang."

"Mr. Phillips?" Rachel replied, stunned.

"I presume it was anyway," the teacher shrugged. "Tony ran over to him shouting daddy, so, I guessed it was his father. There's nothing wrong is there?"

Rachel tried to contain her worry. "Yes. Yes, something is wrong... Especially if it *was* his father."

"If it helps, I heard them say they were going to the park."

Rachel didn't want to hear anymore. Without a word of thanks or even a goodbye, she turned and ran from the schoolyard.

The park was filled with children at play. With all the schools having ended for the day, those who didn't have to be at home were here. Laughing and playing. Footballs were passed around, bikes skidded, as Rachel rushed through the groups, desperately looking for Tony.

Mr. Phillips? she thought. *No, that's impossible. He wouldn't just show up after three years, having run away from them. Not like this.*

Long after the disappearance, Tony had maintained the same story. That there was a bright light, and his father went flying into the sky. The children's psychiatrist had said that it was textbook dissociative disorder, where his mind had invented a new scenario to replace the traumatic one that he must have seen.

The police had no idea where Sam went either. As no laws had been broken, all they could suggest was that they class him as a missing person and keep an eye out. With no evidence of a crime, they had to assume he just left his family of his own accord.

As for what Rachel thought, she had accepted that her marriage hadn't been the strongest before he disappeared. So, maybe he ran off with someone to another country. Somewhere far to get away from the responsibilities he had here. From the debts he left them with. From the pressures of raising a child.

"Tony!" she shouted, running down one of the numerous interconnecting paths, drawing nervous smiles from the bystanders who stared at her anxious behaviour.

"Tony," she cried out again, seeing a small blond boy, facing away from her.

It's him! She thought.

But when she got to the boy, grabbed him by the shoulder and whirled him around, she immediately saw her mistake. This was just a boy who didn't look remotely like Tony, staring at her, terrified.

"I'm so sorry," she said, carrying on down the path and trying to stare everywhere at once. Looking around at every child she could see.

Approaching a small hillock, she ran up to get a better vantage point to see over the park, but when she got there... she stopped in her tracks.

At the far side, twenty feet away, two figures stood staring at the setting sun.

A man, facing away from her, holding a small boy's hand.

Then she heard it; her son's laughter.

"Tony!" she screamed.

The small boy turned and saw her running over.

"Mummy!" Tony smiled before looking up to the man. "Daddy, look, it's Mummy!"

Rachel's expression of desperation turned to relief, then to sudden anger as the man turned to her.

"*SAM?*" she said, aghast.

"Hello, Rachel," he replied, innocently.

"*What the fuck are you doing here?!*"

"Mummy!" Tony gasped in surprise. "You swore!"

She stared at the man she once called her husband. He was wearing a jacket over a pair of blue overalls, wearing workman's boots. A far cry from the well-turned-out man she remembered.

"You've changed your hair." Sam smiled. "It looks very nice."

She reached and grabbed Tony's hand from his father.

"Changed? You've a bloody nerve! That's not all that's changed," she seethed. "You're unbelievable. You ran away for three years. *THREE YEARS*! And you just show up now and steal Tony out of school and—"

"Isn't it great, Mummy?" Tony interrupted, still in awe at his father's reappearance. "Daddy's home now!"

"*Home?!*"

"Come on Rachel," Sam said, holding his hands up. "Calm down. Let's not make a scene. We have a lot to discuss."

Rachel stared at him, full of rage. "You can't just turn up! You *can't* do this!"

Sam's reply was calm, yet detached, at total odds

with her fury. "But you're my wife. Tony is my son…
Let's just go home."

Rachel stood there, at a loss, as Tony grinned like a
Cheshire cat.

The apartment door opened, and Rachel walked in,
still in shock. Every instinct told her to send him away;
to slam the door but Tony's happiness was forefront in
her mind. She couldn't crush that, not now. Not when
her son finally looked happy again. Whatever Sam had
done, she told herself, she could manage it for a few
days. Just long enough to understand what had really
happened to him.

Tony followed, pulling his father in by the hand,
into the hallway where he excitedly looked up
at him.

"Daddy, wait here!" he exclaimed before running
off to his bedroom.

Rachel stared at Sam in the open doorway, smiling.
But it was not Sam's smile. Not the smile she
remembered. It was thin, weak and forced.

She didn't know what else she could do, so she
motioned him to come in.

He stepped over to the hallway mirror and caught
a glance of his reflection. He rubbed his chin, his
stubble.

Rachel saw this too and found it strange he had
hair that he never allowed to grow before. Stubble that
he was almost obsessively shaving before. *'Facial hair is*

for yobs and communists,' was a phrase she had heard him say more than once.

Their marriage had fallen by the wayside just after Tony was born. Sam had lost interest in either of them. He had become more insular. Leaving on work trips more and more often. Staying later at the office. Becoming crueller in things he said about others. And now he stood there rubbing his chin, and she didn't know what else she could say.

"There's a razor in bathroom, if you want to shave that off?" she said, before turning to the kitchen. "I need a drink... Guessing you want a scotch?" She didn't wait to hear his answer.

From his bedroom Tony reappeared, holding the snake in his hand. Letting it slither between his fingers.

"Daddy! You just *have* to meet Harry!" He turned to the snake. "Harry, meet Daddy."

Sam looked at the creature as Tony thrust it into his hand.

"You can hold her, she likes that."

The snake slithered from Tony's fingers onto Sam's. But as it did, its movement became slightly erratic. His head twitched around, as if it could sense what hid under Sam's skin.

Sam found the creature fascinating as he held it firmly, and admiringly held it close to his face.

"Daddy?" Tony asked, suddenly serious. "Are you back for always? Are you coming back?"

"I think so," Sam replied, still meeting the snake's gaze.

"What about Joe? Is he leaving?"

With some confusion Sam turned to his son. "Joe?" he asked.

Rachel had two glasses in front of her. With ice cubes in both, one had gin, the other scotch.

She stared at them for a minute, before downing her gin, then the scotch.

Both measures downed quickly and now left their burning trail down her throat.

Neither of the drinks helped, yet she repoured them anyway.

Grimacing, she couldn't help but hate what was happening now.

She walked over to the phone on the wall and quickly dialled. Keeping an eye on the doorway, she spoke quietly as the line was picked up.

"Stan? It's Rachel. Can you put Joe on?"

The minute it took for Joe to pick up the phone seemed like an age, and Rachel expected Sam to suddenly appear from the hallway.

"Joe? Hey... Are you sitting down?" She said, hushed. "Yeah? Sam's back... Hang on." She quickly put the phone down and closed the kitchen door, knowing Sam would probably still be there.

She went back to her call. "Hi... Yeah, he looks bloody awful. Just like... I dunno... Seedy? Yeah that.

And it seems that he's conveniently lost his memory. Acting like all is well and back to normal... Yeah, please. If you can get here as quickly as you can... Okay? Sure, I love you too."

Sam was no longer in the hallway, having been led to the living room by Tony, who now sat on the sofa next to him. Sam still held the snake in his hand, looking at the animal skittishly darting over his fingers.

"Why is she called Harry?" he asked.

"Harry, short for Harriet!"

"Ah!"

Tony looked proudly at his pet. "She's laid four eggs already!" he said. "Do you know how long they take to hatch?"

Rachel, off the phone, was about to pick up the glasses when Tony opened the door, running in.

"Daddy said Harry's eggs could hatch at any time!"

"Tony, come here," she said. "Listen... About your father." She made sure to quickly check the hallway to make sure he was not listening. "He's been away a long time, you understand. Things have changed. They cannot just be as they were."

Tony wasn't listening though. "Daddy said everything's going to be fine! We are all going to be together."

Rachel sighed. He didn't want to break his heart

but also couldn't have Sam waltzing back into their lives.

"I'm going to show Daddy Harry's house," he said, running back to the door, before looking back. "Are we having fish fingers for dinner?"

"I guess... Sure," Rachel replied, with cooking being the last thing on her mind.

6. EGGS

When Rachel walked into the living room with the drinks in her hand, Tony had already dragged his father away.

His jacket was slung over the back of the chair, which she walked over to and picked up to hang on the coat rack. But as she grabbed it, a few things fell from the pocket onto the floor. A wallet, a few folded pieces of paper and a photo.

A photo of Jane Baker.

A woman whom Rachel didn't know or recognise.

A woman who was killed in her car the night before, along with her husband and child.

Harry was placed back into the small vivarium as Tony spoke.

"She loves it when I sing to her," he said. "I try to sing her a song a day."

Sam was not really listening. He was standing in

the middle of the room looking around at the boy's possessions. The toys. The schoolbooks. The circus posters cluttering up his walls.

Rachel's voice called out from the other room. "Sam, can you come in here please? We need to talk."

"Your drink!" she said curtly, pointing to the glass of scotch on the coffee table. Her emotion and nerves were evident from her expression.

"Are you upset?" Sam asked walking in.

"What the *fuck* do you expect me to feel?" She grimaced in a whisper. "You disappear for three years. *Three... damn... years.* And what? Am I supposed to be grateful? Glad you're back? Happy you decided to swan back into our lives?"

He didn't react. He was calm in his reply. Too calm. "Who is Joe?"

Her laugh was unintended, but from her gut. "What business is it of yours? Huh?... If you *must* know, it's Joe. Joe Hayward. My photographer... But what about you? Who have *you* been with?" She picked up the photo of Jane Baker that fell from his jacket and tossed to the table by his drink.

He looked down at it and shook his head, lying as best as he could. "I can't tell you who, where or what I've been doing." He glanced back up her, speaking in an almost monotone. "I remember us... At the cottage... I was playing with Tony... And then it got very dark. Then the sky burned bright and hot. I tried to hold on, but it pulled me up toward it... That's all I know. All there is."

"You just disappeared!" she retorted. "You ran away!"

"First thing I remember is standing outside the school, seeing Tony."

"So?" Rachel said. "Doesn't matter. Life went on. *I* went on. I'm happy now. Finally!... So, what are you going to do?"

"Do? This is *my* home."

"Yours?" she scoffed. "It's been in my name since the day I paid every penny for it. Same with the cottage. What did you ever contribute? Anyway, I'm with Joe. And this is *his* home now."

Miss Goodman heard the front door slam in the lobby.

She peered out and saw Joe running up from the lobby.

"Ah Mr. Hayward, I see you're running up the stairs again," she called out sarcastically.

"Sure am Mrs. G," he said with a smile. "It helps me get to my apartment." He didn't wait for a reply to his joke as he carried on up the next flight of stairs. "Bye," he added.

With an indignant grunt, she scuttled off back inside her home, closing the door behind her.

She tottered along the hallway to her loving room. This apartment had an identical layout to Rachel's apartment above, but this one was darker and over furnished with antiques, throws and cushions. On her windows, the curtains never opened, and the home lived by lamplight, where the time was hard to ascertain.

The television was playing a loud quiz show, with all the colourful flashy lights and an overly confident presenter.

Beside a high-backed chair that was in front of the screen, a small wicker basket sat, where an old, crippled Dachshund dog slept. He wore a disposable nappy around its low half.

"He is a vile man you know," she said to the dog. "Isn't that right my Willy-Willy William?"

In reply, the dog didn't look up, wag its tail or even take notice. It just let out a long dribbly fart. One that was full of other gifts.

Grabbing the box of nappies from the side, Mrs. Goodman shook her head.

"I swear you just do that to tease me."

The dog may have lost its bowel control in its advanced years, but Mrs. Goodman didn't really mind. She was happy to have something to do. Someone to rely on her. A purpose.

Joe had planned to just walk in and not say a word. He knew that nothing good could come of getting involved, so made a promise to himself that he would keep quiet until Rachel needed him.

He forgot that plan as soon as he strode into the

living room and saw Sam, scotch in hand. Dressed in overalls.

"Well, well," he said. "The wayward stranger returns!"

Sam looked at Joe without emotion. "I hear you've been seeing to things whilst I've been... gone."

Joe didn't really know Sam much before he had disappeared. He was just his boss's husband. Someone who sat miserably at staff get-togethers. Someone who Rachel complained about all too often.

"Seeing to things?" Joe scoffed, walking over to Rachel. "By that you mean paying the bills and being in love with the woman you abandoned... then sure... *Seeing* to things... So, what brought you back then? Ran out of money? Bored? Dying?"

Sam didn't reply, nor look like he had any emotional reaction to any of it. He just looked at Joe the same as if he were a fly buzzing around. A mild annoyance.

Rachel, though, was tightly gripping her nearly empty glass. She was trying her best to not overreact to any of this.

"Joe, can you give me a hand in the kitchen for a sec?" she asked, dragging him out and leaving Sam on the couch.

Joe went straight over to the fridge and took out a can of beer. Cracking it he took a swig.

"What's with those overalls?" he said to Rachel,

who was refilling her glass. "He looks like a bloody mechanic."

She shrugged. "I dunno. Not about any of it... What do you think? He said he doesn't remember a thing. Nothing since he turned up at school today."

"Me? No idea. But it sounds like bullshit. Tony said that too this morning you know. Like father like son." He walked over and went to kiss her, but she backed away.

"What? I can't kiss my girlfriend now?"

"I'm sorry... But it's just so confusing him being here. I don't want him here at all—"

"Good," Joe replied in relief. "I was worried you'd ask him to stay or something."

Rachel closed her eyes for a few seconds. "But I have to remember, he *is* still my husband."

Joe's smile fell away. "You haven't seen him for *years*. And even before that, you said he treated you like shit." His shoulder slumped as his voice raised. "You can't still be in love with him, surely?"

"God no! And I didn't say that! Please keep it down!"

Joe paused for a moment. "Wait. Where's Tony?"

"I told him to go to his room while we sort all this out."

"Right." Joe couldn't face the rest of his drink, as he placed it on the counter. "Jesus, I bet that kid's out of his mind with delight."

. . .

Sam hadn't waited in the living room, but walked back to Tony's room, where he now sat on the bed, with his son perched on his knee. The raised voices from the kitchen could be heard as muffles through the wall.

"He's angry," Tony said worried. "I hope Mummy isn't angry too."

"There was a girl with you this morning," Sam asked, not caring about the domestic issues. "When you went to school, who was she?" He also didn't care that this question proved he was lying to Rachel about his memory.

"Analise? She lives here and looks after me when Mummy and Joe go to work," Tony smiled, having no clue of the lie. "She's going to teach me French as well!"

"Tell me, how long has she been here?"

Before he could answer, the bedroom door was pushed open. Rachel was there looking tired and emotional.

"Tony, time for your dinner?"

Grumpily Tony moaned. "No! I want to stay with Daddy!"

"Go on," Sam said, lifting him off his knee. "You go and eat... I'll be here when you get back."

With a sulk, he stomped out of the room.

When they both left, Sam's attention soon moved back to the vivarium. To the heated tank with moss, to Harry who was coiled on her eggs.

Walking up to it, Sam stared down at the small habitat, as he slowly put his hand inside. He quickly batted the snake out of the way, and he reached down to four small eggs, then lifted them out. Harry meanwhile was twisted around in a panic at her stolen children. Having no venom or teeth, she was helpless to stop this attack.

Sam didn't care about the snake's upset. He just focused on the first egg. Their translucent shells were thin and parchment like. Inside of each, a small lump sat incubating.

He lifted the egg up to his mouth and gently sucked at the end. A light pop sounded as the shell broke, and he noisily ate out its living contents.

With a satisfied smile, he moved to the second egg.

As he lifted it up, and sucked at its end, popping the same way as the first... but he didn't notice Tony there in the doorway.

The young boy had come back to ask his father to come to the kitchen and now was transfixed in horror at what Sam was doing.

For the first time since he arrived, an emotion entered Sam: shock. He dropped the remaining eggs to the floor, and they landed with a breaking squelch.

The front door opened as Tony ran out of the building in floods of tears.

From the kitchen, neither Rachel nor Joe had heard as they were busily trying to work out what to do. Though Sam had heard and was now in pursuit.

. . .

Tony was already a flight ahead as he ran down the stairs.

As he got to the lobby, he didn't head outside but kept running down to the next level. He was in too much of a panic to think much about where he was going.

Behind, Sam whirled down the steps. Hearing Tony's cries ahead, they were the only clue that the boy had ran down to the lower level of the building.

Getting to the bottom, to a glass paned door marked 'Caretaker', he shouldered it open and walked inside.

This basement level was dark. With a large boiler, a garbage chute collection trolley, and a large metal rack of tools, paint cans and other assorted cleaning and maintenance essentials.

In the same darkness, as Tony silently squeezed into the space between the boiler and the wall, the boy couldn't see a thing. He could only hear his father talking from the other side of the room.

"Tony," he called out. "Don't be scared, Tony. You're not in trouble... Really."

At the bottom of the boiler, the furnace kicked in as it automatically ignited, causing Tony to let out a surprised yelp.

Hearing this, Sam stepped nearer.

Through the small glass on the boiler door, the now ignited fire filled the room with a glow.

"Come on out of there," Sam urged. "You don't have to hide from me... I'm your dad... Your *real* Daddy. We are the same you and I."

From the darkness, Tony's small voice came out. Tearful and whimpering.

"Were you really in prison?"

Sam stood by the boiler, waiting for the boy to emerge. "Prison? Who told you that?"

"People at school..." he wept. "But Mummy said that you were on holiday forever. That you left us."

Sam paused for a moment before answering. His words slow and careful.

"I haven't been on any kind of holiday, and I was not in any prison."

Crouching, he looked down the small gap, to where Tony hid in the murky fire lit gloom.

"I've been somewhere very special... and do you want to know why I came back?" he smiled. "I came back for you. You see where I went, they are connected. And when I went, I was missing a connection. And *you* are my connection. The extension of my life. But as they greatly enjoyed me, they want you too. They need my child to... be part of them. It helps have their own progeny. They need that, you see... Or they can't grow... You must have felt it, the link between us over the last couple of days... I have... But it's not complete you see. It's hard to explain when you can't see all... You do want this, don't you?"

"Yes," came the tiny reply. "But I don't understand—"

There was a long pause.

"Daddy?" he asked.

"Yes?"

"Why did you do that to Harry's babies?"

Sam knew that he was not ready for any truth, so opted for a lie. "Do that? I was trying to help them. They were stuck in those eggs. They were hurting. I tried to get them out... And for that you can't use your fingers, because of the germs... But by the time I got to them, they... I'm sorry to have to tell you... They all died."

That reason made no logical sense, but to Tony it was all he needed to hear to quell his fear. His father tried to help the small snakes, yet they all died. Tony's mind chose to ignore the strange tongue. Ignore the pleased expression on his father's face. Ignore the sucking sound as he ate them. He only saw his father. His father who had finally come home. Come home for *him*. It's what he prayed for, and the trauma took the facts away and showed him only what he now wanted to see.

"Do you promise?" Sam asked. "To keep this a secret? That you're coming with me?"

"Cross my heart and hope to die," Tony replied, getting to his feet and walking out of the narrow space.

"Deal. It's our special secret. Just between us," Sam reached his hand. "Let's go back upstairs before your Mummy wonders where we've got to."

7. PROGENY

Rachel and Joe had no idea that Sam and Tony had gone anywhere.

When Tony returned, he sat back down at the table and continued eating his fish-finger dinner. Meanwhile, Sam was in Tony's room gathering up the fallen eggs, munching the last of the embryos.

After he'd finished his dinner, Tony changed into his pyjamas and climbed into bed with a comic book, settling comfortably beneath the covers as the adults had their food.

Joe, Rachel, Sam and the recently returned Analise were now sat at the table in the living room. Their meal of beef and potatoes was almost finished. Sam was politely eating whilst trying to hold back his distaste of what he now forced down his throat.

"I think it is all very civilised," Analise said, drifting into French. "C'est sûr... Very civilised.

"What is?" Rachel asked.

"This," the girl pointed her fork at Joe, her then Sam. "This ménage à trois."

Ignoring most of the food on his plate, unable to stomach the rest, Sam spoke up, to stop himself vomiting. "What's that?"

"Why the Madame... Living with her lover and her husband—"

"No, Analise," Rachel interrupted, unamused.

"Bah! You English say that we French are so open about the sex. But you are uninhibited, but in a very quiet, secret way." She giggled. "All of you are very dirty behind closed doors, I am sure!"

The meal continued in an embarrassed silence, until Sam stood up and hurried off to the bathroom.

"I am sorry," Analise said after he left. "I didn't mean to say anything bad."

"It's fine," Joe said. "It's just all a bit strange, that's all. We still don't know what is going on."

The silence carried on as they continued eating, neither one of them knowing what to say. The presence of Sam still here even though he had left the table.

Eventually after a minute, Analise spoke again. "Have you told him about you two?" she asked.

From the hallway Sam walked back in, looking a lot better than he had done before having just vomited the food he tried to ingest.

"What about you two?" He said, sitting back down.

"We're getting married," Joe replied, subtly staking

his claim. "We're going to start our own family together."

"How fascinating," Sam replied blankly.

"More wine, anyone?" Rachel awkwardly butted in. "Or more salad?"

From his bedroom, Tony's voice could be heard, calling out.

"Daddy? ... Daddy?"

Both Joe and Sam instinctively got up from their chairs.

Quickly realising that there was no way that Tony would have meant him, Joe slinked down back into his chair. Something that Analise found quite funny as she took the last bite of her meal.

As Sam left the room, Rachel shook her head. "Joe, you really shouldn't have told him about us like that."

"How else should I have done it then?" Joe asked, clearly exasperated at the situation. "You hadn't told him, and it should have been one of the *first* things out of your mouth, as it changes everything."

"I don't know, but the way you said it seemed like an attack."

Sam peered around the door of Tony's dark room with a conspiratorial smile, which Tony was all too happy to return.

"When are we going?" he whispered as his father walked in, shutting the door then sat on the edge of the bed.

"Soon, soon," Sam replied, smiling, but showing too many teeth as he did. He didn't think this would happen tonight, but with the opportunity, Sam was all too willing. "First, we must do something. Something that'll make you *just* like me. You want to be just like me, don't you?"

"Yes!"

"And you must promise not to be scared, okay?"

"Okay," Tony smiled. "I'll be brave."

"Good," Sam's smile was larger, hungrier. "Now when you're like me, funny things will happen to you. What you think in your mind, will come alive. Your mind will project your wants. You shouldn't be frightened of these things, because they are part of you. Things made of you. Do you understand?"

Tony didn't have to answer; his confusion was clear.

Sam's smile closed. "You will be fine when it happens. Just don't be scared. Because there's nothing to be scared of. And when it happens, you will feel better, and you will understand. You will see it all. And you will *become*. You will find a new clarity. A new mind. A better mind. One that will be part of you and be one *with* you."

"What does that mean? What is going to happen? Can you tell me?"

Sam got up from the bed and loomed over the boy.

"Take your top off."

Tony complied, not understanding.

"Now lie very, very still... Blood of my blood. Host of my host."

Analise was clearing the table as Rachel sat in quiet tears at the table, having let the events of the day catch up with her. Finally unloading her worries on Joe, sat next to her, cradling her hands.

"He's crazy," she said. "He's not said where he's been or what happened to him. Claiming he doesn't fucking remember! He should be in hospital if that's true. But he isn't. He's *lying*. He's so obviously lying! And he's not the same, is he? He gives me the creeps now. He really does."

"If I'm honest Rach, he always gave me the creeps," Joe replied. "But if something bad *did* happen to him, he should be going to the police, not a hospital. Anyway, we should be telling the police. They still think he's missing, right?"

Sam leaned down towards Tony, who was trying his best to be calm, but as his father's mouth opened, and dozens of long filamentous, translucent tendrils descended from his throat, the boy couldn't retain any bravery. It was dark in this room, lit only by the light from the streetlamps and moon, but the tendrils were aglow on their own, bright with post-pubescence.

They may have looked somewhat beautiful with their bright colours, like deep sea creatures Tony had seen on television, but he couldn't hide his horror as the tendrils moved closer toward him. His father's face a distortion of what he remembered.

Tony stared as his father's eyes rolled down, showing his red-orbed, alien eyes, there underneath his human lids.

As they fell nearer, the bunched tendrils sprang apart and attached themselves to different parts of the boy's chest and face.

Tony was beyond fear now as his body trembled and he started to whimper.

"No," he gasped, as each head of the tendril attached to his skin, breaking through it.

He tried to squirm, but Sam thrust his hands out to the boy's shoulders and pinned the boy down. Not allowing him to move an inch.

Through his translucent tendrils, a black fluid began to pass down. From within Sam and into Tony's small, scared body. A fluid that was more than liquid. It was part of the being inside transferring. Passing on part of its life into its host's child. The new host for its offspring.

Rachel walked down the hallway, towards Tony's bedroom.

With its door closed, she placed a hand on the knob, hesitating for a second. Cautiously, she turned and put her ear to the door, trying to listen to what was happening inside.

"Madame?" Analise called from down the hallway. "I shall go for a bath now, d'accord?"

Shocked as if she had just been caught with her hand in the biscuit tin, Rachel stood up straight and nodded. "Of course, good night," she replied too quickly.

"Bon nuit!" Analise smiled as she walked to the bathroom.

Turning back to Tony's, Rachel tried to ignore the worry in her mind. She didn't know exactly what she was worried about, but she felt something was amiss here.

When she finally opened the door to her son's room, she felt relief as she saw Sam, lying on the bed next to Tony. A shaft of warm light came in from the window, bisecting the room, falling across them.

They both look exhausted as they slept.

Rachel walked in, picking up a few strewn items that littered the floor. A toy soldier. A colourful activity book about the circus. A stuffed bear. Placing them on the desk, she smiled, feeling a sudden nostalgia. Not how things were or had been, but how things may have been. Sam never spent much time with his son, but seeing them both asleep now, despite her wariness toward the man, it made her happy to see.

"Hey?" she whispered to Sam as she walked over. She shook the man's shoulder gently, rousing him, careful not to wake Tony.

Sam slowly woke up and groggily got up.

"Let's let him sleep," she said.

She guided Sam out of the room and down the hallway. He seemed disorientated, and each step he took was an uncertain one.

"Are you okay?" she asked, holding onto his arm to give him some balance.

"So... tired..." he replied. Speaking the truth to her for once.

"You're so cold," she said feeling his arm beneath the clothes. "Come on, I set up a bed for you in the living room."

He was shivering as he got to the couch, where a blanket and pillow waited for him. As he lay straight down without a word of complaint, Rachel took the blanket and covered him with it.

She watched him for a few moments, and she saw a fragility she hadn't seen in him before. *Maybe he was telling the truth?* She thought. *Maybe he went through some horrible ordeal but has blocked it out.*

The whole apartment had gone to sleep, as the night settled in.

A sharp crack on the other side of his room woke Tony with a start. The noise was soon followed by the sound of something scraping.

Wiping the sleep from his eye, he turned on the bedside lamp, realising the sound came from the vivarium. From Harry.

He gasped as he saw the tank was filled with a dark mass. One that seemed to be growing within those glass confines. Getting out of his bed, he ran over worried and immediately saw the source of the noise. The glass of the vivarium had a long crack along its front. The scraping sound was that of the two new halves of glass grinding against each other.

Before he got close enough to see much more, the side shattered outward, and from within, a huge, thick snake unfurled and uncoiled down to the floor. Not the small size that Harry had been, but a pythonesque monster.

Tony screamed as he backed away.

Sam's eyes snapped open at the sound, and he leapt up from the couch.

As he got to the hallway, he met Rachel who was struggling to put on her robe fast enough, as she too rushed toward Tony's room.

His door was flung open in a panic, and Rachel saw Tony, on his bed. With a pale look of shock, unable to look away from the broken vivarium, as its glass littered his floor.

The massive snake had gone.

Sam looked in from behind Rachel, observing with interest, but allowing her to take the lead.

"What happened?" she asked, as making her way across the floor, stepping her slippers between the fallen shards.

"It—it was Harry," Tony said. "She was... a giant."

Rachel walked by the vivarium and looked in.

There curled up on one side of the moss was Harry. As she always had been. Small and thin. A far cry from the beast Tony had seen break the glass.

Sam looked at Tony as a small smile crept over his face.

Not seeing this interaction, Rachel bent down and rolled up the rug that covered most of the room, wrapping up the majority of shards, and leaving it on one side of the room.

"Okay, nobody touches this tonight," she said as she kicked a few stray shards to one side. "We will deal with it in the morning."

"Are you cross with me?" Tony asked.

"No baby," she said, taking a long breath in. "I'm just very tired. So, when you get up, put your slippers on or you'll cut yourself. I'll get it all cleaned up, and I'll sort out Harry as well. Get her a new tank, a plastic one this time. She will be okay till morning there."

After Rachel had tucked him back into bed, reassuring him that everything was fine, she and Sam quietly left their son to sleep. No one saw the massive snake slip out from beneath Tony's bed as he lay there staring at the ceiling, then disappear into the darkness beneath the large set of drawers, all whilst Harry remained in her broken home.

Analise lay in the bathtub, having heard the commotion from Tony's room, and not appreciating her quiet being disrupted. When the noise stopped, she shrugged and turned back to her soaking.

Closing her eyes, she tried to relax again, but as soon as she did, a small movement in the water brushed against her skin.

Jolting she looked down and saw a small worm, no more than two inches long, swimming in the water around her knee.

"Urgh!" she exclaimed, disgusted and leapt out of the tub, onto the cold tiles. "Dégueulasse."

But the water worm was not alone. There were two others of the same size swimming in the soapy water.

Staring at them incredulously, she snatched each one out of the bath and dropped them into the nearby toilet.

"Putain, Tony!" she grimaced as she walked over to the sink to wash her hands. "It's not funny."

Tony couldn't go back to sleep; he just lay in his bed staring at the ceiling.

He felt something was different. Something he couldn't place.

After a while, the silence started to feel oppressive to him. Like there should be noise there. Should be *something*. Crickets outside? A fox in a nearby field? But there was nothing.

As soon as he wished he wanted to hear something, a repetitive spinning sound pulled his attention toward the window.

Whirr. Whirr.

Silhouetted, on his windowsill was something that hadn't been there a few moments ago.

Whirr. Whirr.

Maybe he left his clothes on the back of the chair? *No, his clothes were in the wash basket there,* he thought. And what was that sound. That... whirring... still it went on.

What was that?

He switched on the lamp and almost laughed aloud, as there, on the back of the chair by the window, was the last thing he'd ever expected to see.

On the wall beside the window, was one of his posters. One of a Billy the Circus Dwarf from the McGonigal family circus. The circus that had come to town a year ago that Joe and his mother had taken him. She had been working on their advertising campaign at the time and pulled a few strings so he could meet the entire troupe. And Billy was Tony's favourite. He even signed the poster for him.

But that treasured keepsake on the wall was now empty. All that was left on the poster was the backdrop of the big top and the logo of the circus. Billy was missing from the image.

Instead, Billy the Circus Dwarf sat in his room. Perched on the back of his chair, wearing the same big, pointed hat, with the same painted face, with the same brass bulb horn hanging from his belt. Playing with the same yo-yo—the cause of the whirring.

He stood staring at Tony with a wide grin, as he

spun the yo-yo around his body. He put on a skilled display, as the toy whirred up over his hand, around his waist, flicking out and retracting all around him.

The clown then turned to a bookshelf and aimed the yo-yo toward it. It spun with a shriek toward the shelf, stopped just short as it clipped one of the books, then span back into his grasp. The book it hit then fell off the shelf. Flapping onto the floor.

Tony couldn't help but clap with delight. Not understanding what this was, but being lost in the sudden mayhem, felt that it was somehow right.

The clown looked around the room, and seeing the small plastic panther on the desk picked it up and made it walk along, until he set it down to rest and patted its small head, as if it was alive.

Am I dreaming? Tony thought. *No, I didn't feel asleep.*

Did his mother bring in Billy for a late-night show? Impossible. She hated him.

Was he magic? Maybe.

Before he could wonder anymore, the small man dropped from the chair and aimed his yo-yo at the bedside lamp. But this time the yo-yo had changed. No longer was it a rainbow-coloured toy, now its circumference had altered to a dark, metallic collection of spinning razors.

It whirred at the lampshade, slicing into its fabric and leaving a gaping hole in it like a claw mark. The clown then turned the yo-yo razor to the desk chair. Its blades flew, cutting into the wood and destroying it with ease. Within two attacks, the chair lay in pieces of sliced wood, having rattled across the floor.

Tony didn't see any danger in this. It was as if Billy was hearing his thoughts and bringing them to life! He got out of his bed, and walked over to the clown, where both started to jump up and down, dancing the same imaginary song, dancing in surreal delight.

Directly under his room, Mrs. Goodman was in her bedroom wearing an overnight face mask and with rollers in her hair.

Above, the noise had been relentless all night, and just when she thought it was over, she had been woken up again by it. But now it had come back louder, as she heard jumping up and down.

She had no idea what was going on, but she couldn't stand it anymore.

Holding a broom in her hand, she jabbed its handle at the ceiling. Banging repeatedly to get her message across.

Bang, bang, bang, bang.

Tony had never been like this before. Never made a noise that ever woke her. But now, she could hear him laughing and clapping when he should be fast asleep.

Tony and Billy paused as they heard the *bang, bang,*

bang, bang from beneath them. Both stared at the floor, then to each other.

Billy looked confused and shrugged.

"That's Mrs. Goodman," Tony whispered. "She smells."

Familiar footsteps in the hallway then grabbed their attention.

"Quick!" Tony said, leaping back into his bed. "It's Mummy!"

Billy smiled as he threw the yo-yo toward the desk lamp. The spinning razors flew and severed the electric cable with ease. With a flash and a noisy spark, the room was cast back into darkness.

Rachel, having been woken by her son's laughter, was in the hallway, still half-asleep. There was no more noise, but she wanted to check that all was okay.

She opened the door as quietly as he could and peered inside.

There, Tony was lying in his bed, his eyes squeezed shut. Obviously not asleep.

"If I hear one more squeak out of you tonight," she said. "I'll... I'll be very angry. You understand?"

Slowly, Tony opened his eyes and looked guiltily at his mother.

"Tony? Understand?" she added.

"Yes, Mummy," he said.

With a nod, Rachel closed the door.

· · ·

As soon as she did, she heard a thud, as something slammed on the door from the inside. She was about to rush in as shout, but she was exhausted to care. Too exhausted to deal with it. Instead, she walked off in a huff, heading back to bed.

Down the side of the bookshelf, having hidden from view, was Billy. He peeked out, with a length of string extending between his hand and the yo-yo, which now sat embedded in the bedroom door. Its razor gouged deep into the wood. Right where Rachel's face was moments before.

He chuckled as he yanked on the string. The weaponised yo-yo span back into his grip.

"How do you catch it?" Tony asked, amused.

To which the clown removed the yo-yo from his hand and held his palm up. It was dripping with blood. Long, dripping gashes had been sliced into his skin. The razors having bitten into him, upon each return catch. Something they both found funny, as the clown lifted his hand and licked his fresh wounds.

8. PLAYTIME

Joe and Rachel hadn't been able to go back to sleep. They both lay in bed looking maudlin.

"I think we should go to the cottage tomorrow," Rachel said.

"Who should?"

"You, me and Sam." She sighed. "We need to talk all this over, away from Tony and Analise. They boy just distracts Sam."

"Whoa, hold up," Joe sat up. "Talk what over? You just said earlier that you want him gone. What is there to say?"

Rachel shrugged. "I just... what *if* he's telling the truth and remembers nothing? What kind of person would I be just to tell him to fuck off right now? He's the father of my child after all... And going back there, it could trigger a memory. Help him piece it back together. End of the day, he's going to be in Tony's life whether we like it or not. May as well try and help and break the truth to him softly. Not with a bloody hammer."

"So, I'm supposed to sit there whilst you and Sam have a lovely catch up? Sounds like a barrel of laughs laced with dollops of bullshit..." he looked at her for a moment but knew her well enough to see when she was not being entirely truthful. "Wait, you've already decided to go back there with him, haven't you? I literally have no say in it."

"He only said he was looking forward to seeing the place again, so I thought I'd ask you first."

Joe looked away with a grumble. "... or tell me, you mean."

"Oh, come on! Be fair. What if it was you? Huh? Anyway, I've got to get this sorted out. And if you don't want to come, so be it, stay here with Tony. But tomorrow, I'm going."

"No way I'm letting you just going off with that lunatic. He treated you like garbage for years, then poof, vanishes to God knows where. Now he's back claiming amnesia. Even if he *was* kidnapped, by some Russian mafia or someone, and held at gunpoint in a cage for all this time, wouldn't stop the fact that you're much better off without him."

"I'm *still* married to him, you remember that? And yes, it was a bad marriage, but I want to at least do all I can to make it all right. For Tony's sake if no one else's."

Joe looked at her, just wanting to shake some sense into her, but knew it was a losing battle. "You don't owe him a thing, he left you. That's a fact."

"Fine!" Rachel's frustration boiled over her any calmness she tried to cling onto. "But I have a duty towards Tony. No matter what. You know that. Sam has rights. Maybe not to the property, maybe not to you and me, but to Tony. And Tony wants him around." She couldn't help the tears that came.

"Okay, okay lady. You win!" Joe gave in as he reached over and pulled her close. "But just do me one thing. Be careful. He's acting so weird. You see him at dinner. Had a face like we were feeding him shit. Then ran to the toilet and came back all fine. I mean, your cooking's not *that* bad."

She let out a small laugh.

A knocking at Mrs. Goodman's door started at 2 a.m. and didn't stop. A constant *rata-tat-tat*, that hadn't woken her up, because she was already unable to sleep from the earlier noises from above.

After a couple more noisy outbursts from him, ones where she yet again pushed to bang on the ceiling with the broom, she had given up and tried something else instead. She had walked into the kitchen, decided that a glass of hot milk would help her get through the night. One with a generous helping of brandy stirred into it.

When the banging at her door had started, she was at her stove boiling the milk in a pot. And with a tired sigh, waddled out into the hall to see who it was.

The knocking seemed to get harder and more insistent the closer she got to the door.

"Alright, alright!" she griped. "I can hear you... The whole blasted building can probably hear you!

Putting on the security chain, she opened the front door a tiny fraction, enough to see through.

The knocking immediately ceased.

"What do..." her words caught in her mouth, as her annoyance became fear. Fear at seeing the large thing outside her door.

A large shiny pair of bolt cutters slid in from the dark and snipped through the security chain with ease. When it retracted, a large clanking and whirring could be heard.

Mrs. Goodman threw herself against the door, slamming it shut.

"Leave me alone!" she shouted. "I'm calling the police. This isn't funny!"

Whatever was outside heard, and the mechanical sounds quickly stopped.

The sudden ceasing left the old woman at a loss. But not for long, as with a wrenching crash, the lock on the door was cleaved in two as a bayonet speared through the lock's metal plate, destroying it with ease. Inches away from Mrs. Goodman's shoulder.

She yelped, backing away, as the bayonet was pulled back out from the door.

The door flew open as the large thing outside kicked at it.

This was not a man, alien nor clown, but a toy

soldier. A larger, mechanical version of Tony's toy soldier, but this one was not six inches high. It was eight foot tall and moving toward Mrs. Goodman. Its features were moulded plastic, painted with a happy smile. And each movement it made was accompanied by the sound of the machine within it. Clicking and clanking, as the impossible thing lumbered inside—that only moments ago, Tony had imagined happening.

The old lady ran as fast as she could down towards her open bedroom door, but the soldier's plastic hand jerked with a whizz and clank of gyros. To the harpoon gun strapped to its belt.

The soldier dropped to one knee and pulled the trigger. The harpoon fired and streaked through the air, embedding itself in the bedroom door in front of it. The toy then grabbed the attached cable and yanked back. Pulling the door shut with a slam. Trapping Mrs. Goodman in the hallway, unable to escape.

The toy got up again, dropped the gun and was about to advance on the old lady when it heard something. A scratching from the living room door.

William the Dachshund had been woken by the sound and was trying to see what it was.

Distracted from the old lady, the toy backed up against a wall, and reached down to its belt, grabbing a large plastic knife.

Mrs. Goodman didn't waste time; she crossed over to the kitchen and rushed inside. Slamming the door shut, it grabbed the toys attention yet again.

She rushed over to the stove, to the pot the milk

starting to boil over. She reached for a cloth and grabbed it.

Before she had any more time, the door behind her was literally obliterated, as the toy soldier barged its way through the wood. Splintering it into many pieces.

She turned to the toy and threw both the milk along with the pot, straight at it.

With fast reflexes, the soldier caught the pan in its hand.

The *boiling hot* pan in its *plastic* hand.

Mrs. Goodman scrabbled at the door to the fire escape, desperately trying to open the bolts that had lain untouched for many years.

The toy examined its hand, which had totally melted at the contact with the heated metal. The pan now dangled from a long blob of plastic that was its fingers, before stretching down, snapping off and hitting the floor.

The first bolt unlocked, but before Mrs. Goodman could reach for the second, the soldier swung what was left of its melting hand at her.

The dripping plastic flew out and collided with her neck, wrapping itself around. Burning into her skin on contact.

As the plastic throttled her, the toy pulled back its arm with a terrible violence. Not only snapping her neck but ripping off her whole head in one swift move.

. . .

As the sun broke over the city, flooding the streets with its muted rays, most people were just getting ready to leave for work, but Rachel Phillips and Joe Hayward were not. They were on their street by the open car, loading in three overnight bags and a box of groceries.

Joe walked around to the driver's side door. Looking up, he saw a freshly showered Sam, walking down the steps from the apartment block, dressed in a chunky knitted jumper and blue jeans.

"They fit okay?" Joe asked. Trying his best to remain cordial.

Sam nodded, glancing at his clothes. "Thank you, yes."

"Well I never," Rachel laughed. "We finally got Sam Phillips in a jumper."

If Rachel or Joe had paid any real attention, they would have seen that Sam had no idea what she was talking about.

"The man who always told me that jumpers were too feminine for a real man to wear."

Sam nodded with a shrug. "It's nice."

"It suits you," she continued.

Joe had been explicitly told by Rachel to keep his snide comments to himself, but some he couldn't help but say.

"Of course he likes it, Rach, you know Sam and I have the same taste. Quite cozy."

With a roll of her eyes, Rachel got into the passenger side. Sam following into the back.

With the doors closed, Sam looked at Joe.

"I do appreciate this, Joe... really I do," Sam said, wanting nothing more than to end his life, but enjoyed toying with this life form a bit more.

Joe, looking at him in the rearview nodded with a smile. Perceptively not believing a word being said yet not feeling the actual threat.

Rachel wound down the window and glanced up at their apartment. From their living room window, Tony and Analise leaned out waving.

An hour after they left for the cottage, Tony and Analise were sitting at the breakfast table in the kitchen.

Rachel had reminded her that Tony needed to eat more vegetables and to keep the sweets to a minimum. Of course, that request was ignored, and almost immediately bowls of ice-cream and popcorn were laid out as a feast.

"I could eat this for every breakfast," Tony smiled, as he swallowed a large spoonful of ice cream, some dribbling down his chin.

Analise laughed. "If you did eat this all the time you would get spots, and your teeth would fall out."

"I already have a spot," Tony said, pointing to a tiny pimple on his chin.

"Then that spot will get a spot," she retorted, as he went for a second helping. "Or I could get you some fruit if you like?"

"Eurgh," he grimaced shaking his head.

Despite what he said, Tony could feel that something was wrong. The ice cream he ate no longer tasted as good as he remembered. In fact, it was tasting quite acidic. And his thoughts felt fuzzy, like they were covered in cotton wool. He tried to shake it off. He loved ice cream, he always had. He must be wrong.

"How about we play hide and seek?" he said.

"But you're too old for that baby's game, non?"

"I want to, please?"

Analise shook her head. "Ah, you cannot do that here. This house is small. You have living room, kitchen, three bedroom and a bathroom. Where can you hide where I won't find you immédiatement? Anyway, I have to lie down. I have a bit of a headache. So, later, okay?"

The buzzer at the front door rang, making her smile.

"You keep eating, I'll just see who it is, d'accord?"

As the door opened, Michael leaned in to kiss Analise.

Pulling back, she shot him a playfully angry look. "Go into my room," she whispered... And be quiet. I will be there in a moment."

Nodding, he tiptoed in, letting his hand drift around to her front, brushing against her nipples.

"Tony?" Analise said from the kitchen doorway. "Will

you be okay for a while; I have to do some work. We can play hide and seek later, okay?"

With a disappointed nod, he muttered, "I guess."

"Bon, see you in a couple of hours, okay?"

As she left, and he heard her bedroom door close, Tony sank on his stool. Putting the spoon back into the ice cream bowl, not wanting any more.

He just wanted someone to play with. Someone to laugh with. But instead, he had been left alone. Maybe he would watch some television?

And on cue, *Parp, parp!* came the sound of a brass bulb horn.

Tony whirled in his seat and smiled. There sat up on the sink was Billy the Circus Dwarf, with his horn in hand, and a wide mouthed smile on his face.

In her bedroom, Analise heard the horn.

"Pfft, these children, always watching television," she said, dismissing the noise, as she took off her blouse and walked over to the bed.

Having escaped the urban sprawl, and through increasingly smaller towns and villages, the car now travelled through a wild countryside. And from the moment since they had left, not one of the passengers had spoken a word to each other.

Rachel had fallen asleep in the passenger seat, Joe was busily concentrating on the road as a means of avoiding conversation with Sam, and he was just staring out of the back window at the passing landscape.

Analise lay in a post coital glow, naked on the sheets, as Michael lay next to her, still erect and ready to go once more. Their clothes were strewn with haste across the floor.

A light knock then sounded at her door.

"What is it, Tony?" Analise sighed. "I'm very busy."

"Will you play hide and seek now?" came the small request.

"No... later on, okay? I promise."

The pause that followed made Michael stifle a chuckle. "You broke his heart," he whispered to Analise.

"No," Tony eventually complained from the hallway. "I want to play *now*."

Analise looked at Michael with raised eyebrows. Shocked at the boy's sudden outburst. "He's not usually like this," she said under her breath.

Then came another knock.

"Can I come in?" Tony asked.

"Non," she replied loudly as she got out of bed. "I'm lying down."

"But you're *always* lying down!" he replied.

She rolled her eyes. "Okay, fine! Just *one* game, okay? A quick one."

"Oh goody!" came the reply.

She shook her head as she threw on her dress, turning turned to Michael. "You stay here, I won't be long," she said, pointing to his erection. "And keep that ready!"

"Sixteen... seventeen," Tony counted from the far corner of the living room, his eyes squeezed shut. "Eighteen... nineteen... twenty! Ready or not, here I come!"

He spun around, eyes open, scanning the room for any sign of his au pair.

Darting into the hallway, with a grin across his face, he had an idea. The closet by the front door. *Of course! That's where she'd be hiding.*

He grabbed the handle and yanked the door open.

But instead of Analise, he found himself staring at Billy the Circus Dwarf, who simply winked at Tony... and then calmly pulled the door shut again.

Tony wasn't shocked, he just giggled and moved on to the kitchen.

One by one, each and every cupboard was opened, even ones too small for Analise to crawl into. And in each one, as Tony looked expectantly, Billy was there waiting. Smiling. Winking. Shrugging. Laughing.

All part of the real game they were playing.

Not a game that Tony consciously knew he was even playing, but from something deep inside that did know. A voice that was not there before asking for more than laughter or a friend, but a voice that asked for feeding. A voice that was wanting to hunt its prey.

The drive to the cottage continued in silence as they hit hour two of the journey. Rachel was still asleep as Joe turned the car down a country lane, heading towards the hills overlooking the cottage.

Tony walked from the kitchen to his mother's bedroom and was starting to get annoyed that he hadn't found Analise.

Lifting the valance, he stared under the bed, but all there was were a few boxes and a suitcase.

Behind the curtains, nothing but window.

Moving over to the fitted wardrobes running the length of one wall, he unlatched the concertina-style door and pushed it open. The panels clunked against each other like dominos as they whole side opened, exposing Rachel and Joes clothes.

Appearing from under the bed, where he hadn't been before, Billy put a finger to his lips as he gingerly tiptoed to where the coats were hanging. He pointed at them with a mischievous smile.

Tony crept over, seeing dozens of pairs of shoes on the floor with long coats hanging down over them. But one pair of shoes were unlike the others. Ones that belonged to Analise.

Starting at one end of the coats, Tony thrust his hand in.

"Getting warm…"

He moved his hand between the next coats.

"…warmer…"

The next.

"… It's getting hot!"

And the next.

"… so boiling!"

He arrived at the point where the leather ballet flats were poking out from a grey trench coat.

At that point his mind faded away, and something below emerged. He lunged in with both hands, grabbing Analise hard by her breasts.

"GOT YOU," he shouted.

"Ow!" she cried, pushing her way out and slapping his hands off from her. "Don't do that."

"My turn to hide," he shouted happily. "Come on, Billy!"

Analise looking confused, as no one else was there.

"Who's Billy?" she murmured.

Analise didn't want to play anymore but had little choice as she was at the far end of the living room, facing the wall.

"Dix-sept. Dix-huit. Dix-neuf. Vingt," she counted aloud in French. "Okay, here I come."

After looking around the living room, she walked out into the hallway, quickly noticing the half-open closet by the front door. Thinking that Tony hadn't even tried, she walked over, took hold of the handle and pulled the closet open.

"Found you!" she exclaimed, but there was no one there. Just brooms and linens.

"Damnit," she said, turning back to the kitchen. Thinking he may be behind the door, where he had hidden when they played last.

As she walked toward it, a noise came from behind her. A scampering of tiny feet, and a click of the door.

Turning, she saw the front door wide open.

"I said stay inside," she sighed loudly.

She got to the landing, just in time to see a small figure running into the lift, and the doors closing behind it.

"Merde," she seethed as she hurried to the staircase, down to the next floor where she pressed the call button hoping to stop it. But she was too late, the lift just passed by.

With an annoyed exhalation, she turned and ran down two more flights to the first floor, where the empty lift now stood with its doors wide open.

Slightly out of breath, Analise approached the open door and looked inside the carriage.

"Tony?"

It was empty.

Turning back, she looked down into the stairwell. Mr. Knight, the irritable caretaker in his seventies was mopping the ground floor lobby.

"Mr. Knight?" She shouted. "Have you seen Tony?"

Without looking up, the old man shook his head and continued cleaning.

"Nice to see you too," she mumbled.

She was about to give up, when a giggle came from the floor above.

Though not liking lifts, she was also too tired to climb the stairs she had just ran down and gave herself no choice but to opt for the easiest option.

She stepped in the lift, closed the grate and pressed the button. She was confused that Tony managed to get past her and run back up to the apartment and had no idea how he could have done it.

As the doors closed, she looked ahead. She didn't see Billy the Circus Dwarf above her, wedging himself horizontally in the roof of the carriage.

With a cruel grimace, the clown let go.

The apartment door was open as Billy exited the lift smiling, dragging the unconscious body of Analise behind him.

Tony stood there—or what had once been Tony—delighted at the capture, clapped his hands with joy, as Billy kicked the door shut behind him.

Motioning to Analise with an outstretched hand, Billy's grin was almost as wide as his face as Tony sat astride Analise's stomach. Without any fear he reached out and grabbed her breasts. Squeezing them.

At the same time, Billy twice sounded his horn. Each *parp* going along to each squeeze, making Tony laugh out cruelly.

As he squeezed some more, Analise started to come around. Her moans soft at first as her eyes began to flutter.

From behind his back, Billy produced an oversized mallet, and with a whoop, smashed Analise hard over the head, breaking the skin and knocking her out cold.

Tony's hands started to caress more and he leaned forward, and from his mouth, a slender black mass unfurled. A collection of proboscides just like his father's. His real father's. But this was not for the same purpose. This new Tony had a full stomach. Not of food or dessert, but of something much worse.

The tendrils hung down and found Analise's navel. Playfully working around her stomach until they ventured in, disappearing into her skin the closer Tony moved down. From within his gut, a thick sludge came up. Bloating each proboscis as they delivered their payload under her skin, skittering darkly across her belly until they disappeared beneath.

From Analise's bedroom, Michael was having a cigarette as he heard a thumping sound.

9. RETURN

The cottage sat at the end of the muddy lane, as Joe let out the breath, one that he felt he had been holding since they left London. Outside the gate, he pulled the car to a stop and turned off the ignition.

Rachel, who had woken up only a mile back, stared in alarm at the cottage, at front door now being wide open.

"Oh shit!" she said. "Someone's been here."

"Burglars?" Joe asked.

She didn't answer as she got out of the passenger side and opened the gate.

Joe got out and trailed behind as they walked up the path. They hadn't visited here for a long time, as was evident by the large overgrowth of weeds that sprawled across the garden.

Pushing the cottage door fully open, Rachel was immediately confronted by a pungent smell. She didn't see the mark burned into the paint on the front door, the one the same size as Sam's hand.

"Ugh, its gas," she said, covering her mouth with her sleeve.

Waiting for a moment to let out some of the polluted air, she entered. Joe behind her, with Sam still watching from the car.

Opening the kitchen door, the gas smell became much more intense. She walked in and saw one of the valves were open on the stove, so turned it off. Not that it mattered, the gas supply had been depleted.

Coughing from the toxicity, she unlocked and opened the back door, letting the air in.

"I'll go change the cylinder," Joe said, walking through to the supply shed out back.

Rachel methodically opened the doors and windows in all the other rooms. But when she got to the bathroom, she saw a towel discarded on the floor. One covered in a thick, green, gelatinous substance.

"Christ," she said through her held breath. "What the hell did this?"

Before opening anymore of the house, Rachel came rushing to the front door, holding the gloopy towel in front of her, and dropped it into the empty garbage can.

Stubbing out his cigarette, Michael got up from the bed, grabbed a pair of underpants, and put them on.

Another concerting thump sounded, followed by a sliding of something heavy.

Cautiously, he cracked open the door and peeked furtively into the hallway.

"Anna?" he whispered. "Analise?"

Opening the door more, he looked out. The hallway was empty. Stepping silently, he moved up to the kitchen, but no one was there either.

Turning, he walked back in the living room. Each step as gentle as they could be. Not wanting to alert Tony to his presence if he could help it.

But Tony knew, and the new Tony now inside and controlling him knew too.

They must have gone out, he wondered. *But what the hell was that sound?*

Shaking off the worry he turned back but stopped with a gasp.

There in the middle of the hall was a green, mechanical toy tank. Its caterpillar tracks buzzed into operation as it started to move toward Analise's bedroom. The clanking was very high pitched, like a real tank's noises on helium.

Amused, yet baffled, Michael followed the tank to the doorway, intending to pick it up, but as he reached down—

BANG!

The tank fired a very loud round of ammunition from its plastic cannon. It blasted a chunk of plaster from the wall in front, sending a hanging picture crashing to the floor.

"Jesus Christ," he shouted.

As if the tank heard him, it suddenly clicked into gear, its turret turning, as its tracks wound around, turning the machine to face him.

Before it could take aim any aim, Michael darted through the nearest door. The bathroom.

Locking the door behind him, he waited, head against the door listening.

The whizz and clack of the toy outside got nearer and nearer, until it came to a stop outside, falling silent in an instant.

Feeling some relief, he turned around, and what he saw made his breath stop. There was Analise slumped on a bath stool, naked and unconscious, with a trickle of blood dripping from the wound on her head.

Then *BANG!*

The tank's cannon went off again, talking a chunk out of the lower part of the door, narrowly missing his leg.

Snatching up a bath towel, Michael flicked the lock and opened the door wide. As the turret went to turn, he threw the towel over it, blinding the toy. It began to spin under the cover, trying to find its bearings. Its whine of the tracks sounded like a cry from a wounded animal.

Michael reached down, grabbed the towel and flipped the tank onto its back.

As the tracks helplessly span in the air, the toy rocked side to side like a turtle on its back, unable to right itself.

Michael turned to Analise. To her naked body just flopped on the stool. "You're dreaming..." he said, seeing the bizarreness of what was happening. "Wake up... You gotta wake up."

Slapping himself, he gritted his teeth. "Wake up!" he commanded again, as his eyes welled up... but his commands were no use.

"This is *not* a dream," Tony said, appearing by the living room, and next to him was Billy.

Both of whom Michael now saw and immediately feared.

He ran to the front door and opened it, but didn't get a chance to run any further, as through the dark ahead of him, a smear of blackness made him stagger, as something huge swung in at him.

Michael couldn't comprehend the four sharp nails that flew through the air and ripped into the side of his face. They pierced through his jaw, shredding through his skin, tearing across his cheek and obliterating his nose from his face, shattering his skull along with it. For a second, before the blood spewed out, his tongue lolled freely next to the lacerated skin. His jaw hung broken off to one side. His eyeball pierced and dangled on its stalk. But then the blood came out like a hose.

Before he could collapse, the black creature let out a tremendous roar and sprang through the doorway, barrelling into him, sending him flying backward.

Helplessly pinned to the wall, Michael still assumed he was dreaming, as he saw the black panther which now attacked him. He was almost dead as the beast lunged forward, but Michael was thankfully in too much shock to feel what was happening to him. The panther's fanged maw opened wide as it chewed on the remains of his face, chewing into his brain as it dragged his limp body down to the hallway run rug, drenching the fabric in the darkest arterial blood.

As the panther swallowed the lumps of flesh, Tony smiled as he now tasted it too.

Beside him Billy cheered on.

Rachel was behind the wheel of the car as she drove to the nearest phone. The cottage, though a relaxing home away from home, was isolated and totally off the grid. With a generator for its electricity, canisters for its gas, and water filtered from the nearby stream, it was not connected to any modernisation like telephones or fax machines. So, to make a call, she had to travel.

Three miles from the cottage, close to the junction leading to the next town, a pilar box phone booth stood at the edge of the road.

Stopping beside it, Rachel got out, rummaged in her pocket for some change, and dialled.

As the telephone rang on the living room sideboard, the television played a cartoon loudly.

With the noise of the programme, and the buzzing sound that was coming from the kitchen, Tony could barely hear the call. When he did, he glanced at the receiver, and with a shrug turned back to the cartoon, wishing someone else would answer it for him.

In the kitchen, the blender buzzed as it cut up the ice within a brightly coloured milkshake. Blues, yellows and reds blended as Billy the Circus Dwarf was standing on the stool to reach the counter. Pressing his bloody finger on the blend button repeatedly. Enjoying the noise.

The contents of the refrigerator and freezer had been emptied all over the kitchen floor and table. Half-eaten and now discarded, Billy had taken what he needed and was now making a new concoction for his master. Next to it were pieces of face that the panther left on the rug, pieces that Billy dropped into the mix.

Hearing the phone ring, Billy didn't ignore it as Tony had. He couldn't.

Taking his hand off the button, the blender stopped as he jumped up onto the counter. He scampered across to the edge, reached out and grabbed the phone from the cradle on the wall. He didn't say anything into it though, he just placed the receiver down.

"*Analise?*" Rachel's voice could be heard saying. "*Hello? Tony? Are either of you there?*"

Rachel was worriedly looking around as she listened

into the phone, only hearing the loud sounds of the television.

"Can anyone hear me?" she said in a raised voice, trying to be heard over the noise. "Damnit, what's happening?"

Parp, parp, a horn sounded down the line to her, before cutting off with a click.

Billy walked back across the counter to the blender and unclicked its pitcher, now full of bloody milkshake. He walked over to a long glass and poured the colourful gloop, grinning happily to himself.

Unsettled by what she heard, Rachel immediately replaced the telephone and took a small black book from her pocket—a book of phone numbers. Flipping through its pages, she soon found the one she needed. She picked up the phone, deposited a coin and dialled.

The caretaker's room in the block was grubby yet austere. It offered few comforts: a metal-framed bed, a worn couch, and a bookshelf overflowing with paperbacks. The kitchen was basic and bleak. With one bowl, one plate, one knife, one fork, one spoon. Yet Mr. Knight owned four different-sized glasses and a modest selection of booze, ranging from whisky to wine.

A single lamp lit the room as he sat on the couch, reading a biography of Josef Stalin. With only a handful of apartments to look after, his work was light; and by eleven each morning, the communal areas had already been mopped, and the rest of the day was mostly his own. That is, until his phone rang.

Blindly he picked it up, keeping his attention on the page.

"Hello?"

"Mr. Knight? Hello, its Rachel Phillips from number 6."

He quietly sighed to himself, knowing that her calling could only mean one thing: He would have to get out of his chair and do something.

"Could you possibly go check on my apartment? You've got the key, so feel free to go inside... Tony and Analise should be there, but I'm having trouble getting through to them. I'm worried. If she is not there, could you do something for me?"

Mouthing a silent curse to himself, Mr. Knight forced a smile as he spoke, sounding as subservient as he possibly could.

"Delighted to be of assistance, Mrs. Phillips."

As she spoke, he zoned out, hearing her words but not caring at all of any of them.

"Of course, goodbye."

Hanging up, his smile dropped into a disgusted expression. "Sure, leave that little bastard to me. That's all I want to do with my day."

Putting his book down onto the armrest, the

caretaker got up slowly. As he did, his knees clicked, his spine ached, and hips complained, but he was not a man to give into the ravages of age with ease. He pushed through the discomfort and shuffled out of the room.

Replacing the receiver, there was not much more Rachel could do.

There was nothing wrong, she had convinced herself of that, but the niggling doubt in the back of her mind refused to quieten.

As he got out of the lift, Mr. Knight had the keys in his hand, but didn't want to just walk inside the apartment as he had been given permission to do. Instead, he pressed his finger on the buzzer.

No one answered, but he could hear the television inside.

He pressed the buzzer again, for much longer.

Hearing a shuffle, the door then opened a fraction.

Mr. Knight looked down and saw Tony peering out through the gap. Hiding the sight of Michael's decimated corpse on the blood-soaked rug.

"Boy, that French missy with you?" the old man asked.

Tony shook his head.

"Where is she?"

"Gone out," Tony shrugged.

"Well, I spoke to your mother, she tried to ring you, you know?"

"I didn't hear it," Tony lied, though sounding believably innocent.

"Your father, Joe, is coming to get—."

Tony's expression soured as he interrupted. "He's not my daddy!"

"Maybe not, but as your babysitter isn't here, your mother said that you're to stay with me until he arrives, or she comes back. She doesn't want you on your own. Understand?"

Tony thought for a minute, nodded then slammed the door shut.

Mr. Knight stood back, bemused, shaking his head.

"Awful child," he mumbled.

Inside the loud television switched off, and moments later the door opened again, and Tony walked out. Shutting it, and the violence, behind him.

The old man shuffled toward the lift. "Come on then."

"I'm taking the stairs," Tony announced. "Race you!"

With no intention of hurrying, Mr. Knight got into the lift, shut the gate, and pressed the ground floor button. Taking it all in his own time.

Tony flew down the flights, taking two steps at a time, all which Mr. Knight could see through the grating as it approached the ground floor.

"Children," he shook his head piteously. "They never have any respect."

As the door let out a ping and opened, he had expected to see Tony stood there, ready to gloat at beating him in his race. And that would've annoyed the old man enough.

But it wasn't Tony who was waiting for him.

It was Billy the Circus Dwarf.

Mr. Knight was not quick enough to stop the large mallet swinging in and smashing him across the head. He crumpled to the floor without a sound.

"I'm sure it's fine," Joe said as he opened the car door. "They were probably just playing a game with you."

"She's been less and less trustworthy lately," Rachel said, standing behind him. "Not picking Tony up with little notice. Smoking in her room. And thinking we don't know about her boyfriend."

"Don't worry. Even if she left Tony alone, he'll be fine." Joe got in the driver's side. "He's a sensible kid, and I'm sure Mr. Knight will keep everything in check."

"I know, but I think it's time for Analise to go, don't you? This is just the last straw for me. If it was a joke, it wasn't funny."

Joe nodded, then turned to her. "Talking about not trusting people... Sam. Keep an eye on him, okay? I don't like any of this one bit. I'll only be gone a few hours."

"Not like he's changed *that* much. He's still the same narcissistic bugger I married."

"Okay, okay," Joe smiled. "Just take care. I'll be back soon."

After Rachel kissed him goodbye, Joe set off on the long drive back to London to pick Tony up.

Walking back into the cottage, Rachel closed the door and looked around the living room.

"Sam?" she called out.

Walking into the kitchen, she looked over the food on the table. An open bottle of wine sat in front of three empty glasses. Each plate had a ploughman's lunch on—with slices of bread, ham, cheese, pickled onions, and salad. Feeling guilty for asking Joe to leave before eating, she picked up his plate and put it in the fridge, taking his wine glass over to a cupboard.

"Sam," she called out once more. "Lunch is ready."

Still no reply.

She then noticed the back door was wide open.

"Hmm," she murmured, walking over to the window and looking out into the garden.

There, Sam stood on the brow of the hill at the end of the grass. Staring up into the sky, slowly raising one hand above his head.

As he did, a faint hum began to rise from the glass Rachel was holding. It trembled in her grip, the sound singing into a high, eerie note. Like a finger circling the rim of crystal. Startled, she tried to steady it, but the vibration grew stronger. The glass slipped from her grasp and shattered on the floor, the singing cut off mid-note.

Her eyes darting to the window, she saw Sam still on the hill, his right arm now pointing straight upward.

For a heartbeat, everything was still. Then, from behind her, a sudden deafening crash sounded. Rachel screamed as the light fitting had fallen from the ceiling onto the table below. Smashing the glass and crockery, sending wine and food and shards of porcelain over the kitchen floor.

Rachel staggered backward to the doorway, her eyes darting around the room to seek the cause.

From the garden, Sam appeared, placing one hand on her waist, making her scream a second time.

Turning, realising it was him, she flung her arms around his neck and held tight. Out of instinct more than want.

"Are you okay?" he asked.

Trying to calm herself down, she put her hand up and stroked his head. But as she did, she felt his hair moving.

Pulling back, she looked at her hand, and there between her fingers were large clumps of his hair.

"Sam," she said with worry. "What's happening to you?"

"It seems that I'm moulting," he mused without much care. "Quite a mess, isn't it?"

Looking into the kitchen, he then smirked at the mess. Walking past Rachel to the cupboard he took out two wine glasses. Picking up the toppled wine bottle, he poured the remains equally and handed her a glass.

"To your health, my dear," he said with a smirk.

"What the hell are you doing?" She said, staring at him, the mess, then back again. "What's going on?" As she said that, a waft of terrible body odour hit her nostrils. "And Christ, why do you smell *so* bad?"

Ten minutes later, Sam stepped out of the shower having wasted off the stench that had suddenly radiated from him.

Passing the mirror, he caught a glimpse of his back. At the large, blistered patch across it. Where below the translucent bubble of skin, his dark reptilian surface could be seen under sheen of viscous fluid.

"Not much time," he said, reaching back and prodding one of the blisters. As he did a small amount of liquid seeped out from the edge of its damaged skin.

Not expecting him to still be naked, Rachel walked in.

"Sam do you—" she caught sight of his body. "*Jesus, I'm sorry!*" she blurted, closing her eyes. But as she did, she realised she'd seen something wrong on his back and opened her eyes again.

Sam was fast though and quickly pulled on his shirt.

"What is that?" she said.

"Nothing, just an old scar."

Continuing to dress, he buttoned up his shirt, put on his socks. Leaving his underpants and trousers last, making her presence in the doorway very uncomfortable.

"Sam, please, I'm tired of your games," Rachel said, averting her gaze. "You're not telling me the truth about all this. I know you're not. So please... Just tell me."

"Do you really want to know?" Sam asked, pulling on his trousers. "You may not like it."

She stopped for a moment and turned to him. Staring with a hurt concern. "Please. I saw your wallet, and that picture of a woman in it. Who is she to you? Were you with her all this time?"

Reaching into his back pocket he pulled the leather wallet and looked at it. "Oh, you mean this?" he said. "That's not mine. I found it." He tossed it to the floor.

"Fuck's sake, Sam, that's weak. Even for you."

"It's the truth, I'm sorry that it disappoints you."

Rachel didn't know what to say. She was frustrated and angry but couldn't figure out how to get the truth out of him.

Then she saw the shower.

The water hadn't drained, as there in the outlet was a scummy mass of hair. Hair that had fallen from Sam's body and blocked the wastewater from emptying.

"Really? You haven't got anything to say?" she said, walking in and reaching down. Grabbing the clump of hair, she pulled it out of the tub and, immediately, the water began to drain. Lifting the mass, she dropped it into the toilet and flushed. "Because this is all very, very normal, right?"

10. DEPARTURE

The apartment door was opened wide, as Tony heard Joe walking up the stairs.

"Hello," Tony shouted down. "Joe is that you?"

"Thought you were gonna be downstairs with Mr. Knight?" Joe said, stomping up the stairs. Tired from driving and not looking forward to the journey back. "He didn't answer his door."

He got to the top and saw Tony standing there waiting for him.

"Mr. Knight? I haven't seen him today," the boy said.

"He didn't come up at all?"

Tony shook his head.

As Joe got to the doorway, he noticed that the rug in the hallway was missing.

"What have you been doing?" he motioned to bare floorboards.

Of course, Tony would never reply that the bloody

rug was rolled up and shoved into the cupboard. "Just a game I was playing," he replied.

"With Analise?"

"No, she left this morning. Never came back. Said she was meeting a boy."

"Grab your coat," Joe harrumphed, "we're going to the cottage, okay?"

"Will Daddy be there?"

Joe was not looking to replace Sam, but Tony's enthusiasm for the man who had been gone for years, upset him. Tony never did anything except treat Joe with disdain, and he had tried his best to be the boy's friend. So now, he just felt in a constant deflated state. That Tony would never give him a chance. Especially not now Sam was back.

"Yeah, he is," Joe said.

Tony lit up. "Yippee!"

"Okay, two minutes, okay? Just gotta use the toilet."

Walking toward the bathroom, Joe didn't see Tony's sudden panicked expression.

"Come on!" Tony shouted as he ran down the stairs. "No time to wait!"

Joe was left there, needing to pee, but he couldn't let Tony just run off.

He nodded, accepting defeat. "Fine, I'll go on the way," he sighed.

Through the bathroom door, Billy the Circus Dwarf heard the front door shutting, and giggled. With a plastic bucket in hand, he continued the work he had been tasked to do.

Suspended above the tub, Analise was hung, wrapped within thousands of white, silky threads. Each glistening beneath the bathroom light. The strands wound around her body in tight spirals, weaving into a crescent-shaped cocoon that clung to the ceiling like a spiderweb.

Her body was barely visible through its chrysalis's gauze. With only the faintest suggestion of her face seen pressed against the webbing.

The threads that held her were not inanimate though. They trembled faintly, as the whole shell was its own organism. A thing that incubated what had happened inside of Analise. Drops of moisture slid down the outside and dripped into the tub below, where a large number of eggs lay, having been birthed from the bottom of the sac, splatting down from within her shrouded body. The eggs were each covered in a transparent film that surrounded their alien lives inside.

Billy was scooping up these small embryos with his hand, placing them in the bucket that had been balanced on the edge of the tub.

When they had all been collected, he grabbed the bucket and turned to the door.

He passed by Michael, slouched on the closed toilet, and gave him a wave.

But Michael, with his head now just hair at the back and a mess of pulp and shattered bone at the front, was very much dead.

Into the hallway Billy trundled with a spring in his step, while keeping the full bucket level, careful not to spill any of the contents. Getting to the kitchen, he traversed the discarded food and opened the refrigerator.

In the large salad crisper, there was already a wealth of eggs incubating—the first batch he collected. Now Billy opened it once more and poured the second bucketful on top, filling the drawer close to overflowing.

With a pat on the plastic, he smiled proudly as he closed the refrigerator.

As the sun started to set over the cottage, Rachel hadn't got much further with her conversation with Sam. He had spoken in so many vagaries that it left her more confused than before.

She had left him downstairs so she could change after she had cleaned up the kitchen. She was in the bedroom working out what she was going to say, considering how they could fix this whole mess and, more importantly, how to find out the truth about where he had been.

Now in jogging bottoms and t-shirt, she opened the bedroom door and almost collided with a short step ladder. With it placed in the middle of the landing, it sat underneath the open hole into the attic. Sam was stood on its top step with his top half inside.

"What are you doing?" she asked.

"Looking for tools to repair the kitchen light," he replied, as for a moment, his human memories started to bleed through, overtaking the alien. His insides buzzed. His hair was falling out. His human skin felt on fire. And the creature inside was feeling weak.

He hadn't feasted for days and drifted back to collect its strength, leaving the remnants of Sam to drift around the house.

He had seen the broken light and thought instinctively to fix it. But by the time he reached the attic hatch, his mind had gone blank and the thing beneath his skin was crawling to the surface.

"Forget that and come down," she said. "We've gotta talk before Tony and Joe get here, okay?"

He just stared blankly into the dark.

"Are you even listening to me?" she said, annoyed. "Come back down... Sam?"

Slowly he peered down, a scared look of confusion on his face as he saw her. Remembered her. Remembered him. But by now, more clumps of his hair had fallen out of his scalp, leaving flaky and blotchy skin in its place.

"Rachel," he mumbled sadly, as he tried to think.

Rachel could have sworn he had gotten worse since she saw him only ten minutes ago.

"Come down," she said, worried.

Nodding, he lowered his foot, but as he got to the last step, the being within had grabbed control, and his footing slipped, sending him tumbling backward.

There was a loud bang as he fell from the small ladder and collapsed to the floor, hitting his forehead on the banister.

"SAM!" she screamed as she ran over to his unconscious body.

Joe had finally left the motorway as the sun went down and was now speeding along a lane, his headlights on full, with no other traffic around. On either side of him, lines of trees formed a canopy that turned the road into a tunnel with no moon or stars visible through its entwined branches. They passed a stretch of road where a steel drum sat, with the horrific remains now rotting inside.

Beside him, Tony, who had been sat silently happy suddenly winced in pain. "OW!" he said, clutching his forehead.

"Tony?" Joe said.

"...Ow, ow!" Tony whimpered again, but much weaker this time.

Joe immediately slammed on the brakes, slowing the car to a stop as the tyres skidded slightly. Switching on the interior light, he turned to the boy.

"What is it?" he asked, as he reached for Tony's hand and pulled it away. He didn't expect to see the long bloody graze that now sat above the boy's eye.

. . .

On the landing, Rachel was on her knees beside an unconscious Sam, now on his side. She looked over his body with trepidation. Seeing the few remaining tufts of hair on his balding pate. The blotchy skin that flaked away in some places. But most of all, the large graze above his eye from the fall. The graze that exposed something beneath. Something that made her blood run cold. Unnaturally dark, reptilian skin that peaked out from the wound.

Unable to stop her curiosity, she slowly pulled up his shirt, freeing it from his belt, and lifted the back.

There was the mark she had caught a glimpse of earlier, now there in front of her clearly. But it was not the same as it was then. Now it had grown. Spread out over his skin.

Even as she stared at it in terror, a further change was taking place underneath. An undulation of the scaly thing beneath.

Controlling her rising panic, she let go of the shirt and got to her feet. Keeping her eye on him, she moved back down the stairs as quickly as she could.

In the kitchen, the light fixture lay broken on the table, but all the glass, food and wine had been cleared up. Rachel walked over to the drawer grabbed the largest knife, feeling that she needed something.

As she walked back to the door, she glanced nervously back up the stairs, seeing him still laying there, motionless. She was unsure whether she should be worried *for* Sam or afraid *of* him, or whatever it was that was wrong with him. *Could it be contagious?* She thought before opening the door and stepping outside.

On the porch she looked out on the dark track road that ran past the cottage. Either way there were no lights from approaching vehicles.

"Dammit, Joe. Hurry up."

The air was cold, blowing in from over the moors and fields, making her shiver. But as she was out there, she started to think... None of this would be dangerous. Not Sam. Sam may have been a selfish man, but he would never hurt a fly. She must have been mistaken. She must have been too tired... That couldn't have been scales in the cut on his head. Then she had a terrible, terrible thought... He disappeared, only to come back years later and now his hair is falling out, and he has a horrible growth on his back.

Of all the scenarios for explanation that sped around her imagination, only one stood out. Could he have gone away because he was ill and didn't want his son or her to see it? Is his hair falling in chunks because of radiotherapy? Was that thing on his back... cancer? Is he back just to say goodbye?

This thought eclipsed all the other strangeness, as she started to solely believe that it *had* to be the case.

"Oh Sam... Please no," she said, as she turned to go back inside, leaving the front door open. With the knife still absently-mindedly in her hand, she rushed up the stairs.

As her sight became level to the landing, she immediately realised... Sam was gone.

She froze on the step and stared at the empty floor.

Edging her way up the remaining steps she looked around, getting increasingly frustrated by it all.

"Sam?" she said, nervously, as she stepped over to the second bedroom, pushing the door open.

Moving the step ladder to one side, she then walked down to the master bedroom, and looked in.

"Sam, please. I understand," she said slightly louder. "You're ill, aren't you?"

But no one was there.

Into the bathroom, she walked over to the bathtub and pulled the shower curtain open.

"Please, Sam?" she said as she turned and walked out to the landing.

She was about to walk downstairs again, when a large weight fell on her.

Sam had leapt down from the attic opening, growling loudly, striking her on the bridge of her nose with his fist, breaking it on impact. She dropped the knife as she fell.

She screamed as she hit the ground. Blood pouring from her nostrils, running down her chin as her eyes filled with tears. She thrashed at him in confusion, while he continued growling. A growl that sounded like it was made of static.

He threw her against the wall, where she tried to squirm free but only managed to turn around. He then pushed her hard against the wall. Her face painfully pushed against the plaster.

His mouth then opened, and the tendrils emerged.

But they did not just come from his throat. They came from deep inside and now spouted out from every hole in his body. *Every hole.* The proboscides all slithered out and aimed at her body. The ones from his nose, mouth, and ears all extended and wrapped around Rachel's head, as they yanked at her. Spinning her back around so she was facing him again. Her screamed soon smothered as the tendrils entered her mouth.

His trousers then split open as a longer, darker set of proboscides broke out from his penis and anus and wrapped around his body and shot toward her. Breaking through her clothes and into her.

The pain and confusion were all encompassing as Rachel tried to fight against the horrors happening to her.

She punched and kicked against his grip as her body was in torment, her screams blocked, as she felt a foul liquid dripping down her throat.

Then she reached out and her fingernails caught Sam in the face and raked across his skin, cutting through some of the tendrils. She gouged out skin as if it was made of putty, revealing more of his alien nature beneath.

Through her tears, she saw him scream in pain as he let go, clutching his face, as the split tendrils sprayed white liquid.

The tendrils all broke away, leaving her body as he staggered back. His screams turning furious.

She fell to the floor, but quickly scrambled to her feet, turning and ran back down the stairs, straight out the door. As she did, by some miracle, a set of headlights approached down the lane.

"HELP!" she screamed, wildly signalling to the vehicle. She saw Joe and Tony, staring at her through the windscreen, as she got to the car in a frenzy. She banged franticly on the bonnet. Sam's skin still stickily stuck to her hand, splatted with each hit, leaving bloody, lumpy patches on the paintwork.

"We have to go back!" she screamed, as she ran to the side of the car and launched herself onto the back seat. "Please!"

Joe and Tony could only turn to look at her confused.

With blood pouring from her swelling nose, the remnants of Sam's skin on her fingers, her clothes torn, her whole body violated... she was a mess as she started to break down.

"Go! Just *go!*"

Joe didn't ask questions. He nodded as he quickly whirled the car around, spraying up dirt from the gravel. When he pressed the break in mid turn, Tony suddenly opened his door and jumped out.

"NO!" Rachel screamed.

Joe, leaving the car running, ran quickly after. "I'll get him," he shouted as he chased the boy toward the house. "Tony!" he called out. "Come back!"

Joe quickly outpaced the small boy's legs and grabbed him by the arm before he could get to the door. But Tony was frantic as he wriggled and kicked at him, struggling to get out of his grasp.

Neither of them noticed Sam stood there in the doorway. The proboscides had all retracted as Sam stared, with half the skin of his face now torn away, his true form showing underneath.

He glared fixedly at Joe as he opened his mouth wide. Impossibly wide.

A thin, piercing sound grew from the depths of Sam's throat. Growing louder and louder, as his whole body started to shake with violent vibrations.

Joe let go of Tony, and grasped his own ears, which throbbed under the pain of the tormenting scream.

Tony though was unaffected. Acting as if nothing was happening, he walked past his father and into the cottage.

The scream thickened and intensified as it changed pitch, getting higher.

Joe winced as he was battered down with the sound, recoiling from it. With extreme effort he tried to rush at Sam, tried to push him back, but Sam just opened his mouth wider. The horrendous screech quickly got worse, weakening Joe, almost paralysing him.

His body started to shudder under Sam's assault, as his face reddened and he dropped to his knees. He himself started to scream in agony, but it was unheard through the noise being forced upon him.

Sam then leaned down toward his beaten victim, getting his scream closer to his victim's covered ears.

But Joe's hands could do little to stop this. The sound was not only heard but felt through every cell of his body. Like every part of him was getting filled with a pressure that built up and built up and built up, until...

...The top of Joe's skull cracked open with a dull snap.

His cranium opened outward, exposing his pulsing brain matter beneath. The pressure inside finding its only way out, as contents of his head then burst out of the cracked bone. Grey matters and blood splatting over the porch steps.

The slam of the car door made Sam stop screaming, as he looked up and saw Rachel running over, eclipsed in the car headlights.

He laughed as he disappeared back into the house, slamming the door shut as Rachel got to the porch and saw Joe's body convulsing on the floor. A hideous reflex as his brains were laying in ruin around him.

Her screams filled the night, but she couldn't let herself be broken here. She had to find her son. He was more important than everything else.

All thought of explanation, or reason were gone, as she fought her urge to flee.

She rushed to the front door, yanking at its handle. But it was locked. She then threw her weight against it, but the heavy wood didn't budge.

"Tony!" she screamed. "I'm coming!"

Rushing round the side of the cottage, she got to the living room window. The only window still open from the earlier airing of the gas.

She stepped on the long wooden planter beneath it, and clambered over the windowsill, ignoring the growing ache in her belly.

The cottage was quiet.

The room around her was deathly still as she edged her way to the door and looked up the stairs. But a loud crash from the kitchen grabbed her attention. A splintering of wood and breaking glass.

She didn't want to move or make a sound. But she had no choice.

"Tony?" she whispered. "Is that you? Please don't hide from me."

Slowly and softly, she stepped out from the living room, and down the hallway to the kitchen.

Looking in, she saw the back door wide open yet ripped off its hinges. The window had been smashed.

In a panic, she ran across the room, the glass crunching beneath her feet as she sped out into the garden.

"Tony?" She cried, petrified that he was being hurt.

But she saw nothing in the garden. Running out further she looked around and then saw them. Fifty feet away, Sam and Tony, both bathed in moonlight, holding hands.

She didn't think of herself, she just raced after them as they disappeared into a nearby copse.

As she approached the tree line, she paused and looked into its murkiness. She had to hold her breath to listen for any sounds, as her breathing had become too loud to hear anything else.

But all she could hear was the sounds of the night.

"Tony, please," she called out, rushing in.

The further she went, the stronger the pain in her belly.

Running blindly through the trees, she had no idea where she was going. Not until the light appeared ahead, where the woodland thinned into a small clearing. There, a brightness, strangely cold and blue broke through the branches above, shining down.

Slowly, she made her way across a gully, and toward the clearing. But the closer she got, the more the light grew in intensity, right until it was so bright that it hurt to look at.

A sudden eruption then happened. A low booming drone sounded like the deepest horn, as a wind started to slice through the trees. A wind that smelled of metal and rancid meat. A wind that built up suddenly into a blasting gale force.

From within the light, shadows began to flicker as she saw things moving within it.

She could only think of Tony as she ran forward,

battling the gale, gritting her teeth to withstand the bassy drone and harsh glare.

Getting to the edge of the clearing she squinted into the blaze.

There were two figures in the midst of the luminescence.

One large.

One small.

Within the wind, the debris of leaves and dirt from the forest floor flew around, hitting Rachel as she battled to keep her eyes open.

Taking a step forward, she saw the little figure turn to her.

Tony, she thought.

Staggering forward the wind increased, attempting to push her away.

The small figure continued to stare at her as it lifted an arm.

As it did, the light instantly grew brighter and more blinding as the wind got more powerful, gushing around the clearing in a deafening howl.

The light then climaxed into a sudden flash, sending out a shockwave, knocking Rachel far back into the trees.

As she landed, the world went dark, and the wind instantly ceased.

She sat up and stared into the clearing, bleary and confused, as nothing was there. Just the darkness, and the trees.

She then smelled the burning. She looked above

and saw the trees of the clearing had all been scorched. The branches that remained were mere crackling embers, falling as ash to the blackened dirt.

"No, no, *no!*" she wailed, clambering to her feet and hobbling to the centre of the clearing. Her body now in agony.

She stared above, knowing in her heart what this was, but not believing or understanding any of it.

There, above her, the stars twinkled innocently in the clear sky.

She collapsed to the dirt, still staring up, sobbing uncontrollably, as the now stabbing pain throbbed within her belly.

Her screams reverberated through the trees, but no one except the wildlife had heard her.

11. CODA

As the sun came up, Joe's body remained cold and rigid on the porch, and the cottage was left open to the elements.

Rachel had walked back in a tearful daze, got into her bed and slept for two days. The pain in her stomach had increased, and her belly had begun to swell fast, and was now the size of a watermelon.

She didn't remember getting in the car or driving home, but after she did, she found herself in the lobby of her building, staring up the stairwell, toward her apartment.

She didn't smell the stench coming from beyond Mr. Knights door, nor see the smashed in door at Mrs. Goodman's. She didn't know of any of the dead bodies in all the homes of this block. From 1 through 9, each home had seen many impossible things, but now, all was quiet like a graveyard.

She didn't even remember getting in the lift, she just heard the ping as it arrived at her floor.

Crossing the hallway, she staggered as she grabbed the handle to her apartment door, the pain increasing in her stomach.

Before she could turn the handle, the door opened from inside and a small hand shot out, grasping the door's edge.

There stood Tony with a big grin on his face.

"Mummy!" he beamed. "You look wonderful! You simply *have* to come in and meet everyone."

Rachel stared, unsure of what to think or feel, as the boy walked away down the hallway.

Stuck in such a well of shock, nothing here seemed real.

"Am I dreaming?" she asked.

"We're watching T.V.," Tony said with a chuckle, walking into the living room. "You should join us, Mummy."

She walked sluggishly down the hall and stood in the doorway.

There, in front of the television were twenty boys, all staring at a muted film.

"Everyone, look who's here," Tony said.

Then in unison, each child turned to face her.

Each child was the same.

Each child was Tony.

Each child now smiled at her as they stood up.

"Hello Mummy," they all said as one, walking over.

They all then swarmed around her, looked up with an identical expression on their identical faces, hugging her at once.

"Am I dreaming," she repeated, as she looked around the room blearily.

On the sideboard sat Billy the Clown Dwarf, who tipped his hat to her, as the large, black panther padded by. Moving to the couch where it sat down lazily next to a large mechanical toy soldier.

One of the Tony's reached out and took her hand.

"Mummy," he said. "Come with me."

She had no fight as she followed into the kitchen, his hand tight on hers.

"Look," he pointed to the fridge, which was lying open on its side. "My brothers are here."

In the remnants of the salad tray, a batch of the eggs remained unhatched. They sat there pulsating with life, each now the size of a melon.

He led her over and picked up one of the eggs.

"But soon I'll have even *more* bothers," he smiled as he placed one hand on her large, swollen belly.

He handed her the egg, which she took without qualm, lost in a fog.

"I *must* be dreaming," she mumbled as she leaned in closer, seeing the creature spinning in its embryonic state.

"Dreams are real Mummy" Tony said. "What we dream, becomes real... And soon Daddy will return with the rest of our family. He went in the sky to get them."

"I miss you," she said sadly, not hearing a word.

He stared at her curiously and shrugged. "You're a

great Mummy," he said. "Better than Analise. She tasted awful."

She half-heard as she turned to him. "What?"

"Really, she was blergh," Tony said with a look of disgust. "But Daddy said the rest of the people he met were delicious. So, they're all coming back for dinner. But first he wants our family here to grow much bigger. To spread... And you need some help... You need to really become part of the family. We want you to join us. "

Before she could react, the egg in her hands exploded. From within a collection of black, thin tentacle shot out. Gripping onto her face. She screamed as the creature broke out and latched onto her mouth. Pumping and throbbing into her gullet.

Tony smiled, walked back into the hallway, and up to the front door.

"We only have a few years to prepare," he said to himself, before slamming it shut.

XTRO

ON-SET PHOTOS
by Ed Buziak

Christopher Hobbs (visual consultant)

Philip Sayer (Sam), Harry Bromley Davenport and Christopher Hobbs (visual consultant) shooting forest scene in studio

Shooting forest scene in studio

Danny Brainin (Joe) & Bernice Stegers(Rachel)

Anna Wing (Mrs. Goodman), Harry Bromley Davenport and the animal handler giving acting lessons for Harry the snake

Maryam D'Abo (Analise)

Robert Shaye (exec producer), Mark Forstater (producer) and Harry Bromley Davenport goofing around

Peter Mandell (Billy the Circus Dwarf) & Robin Grantham (makeup supervisor)

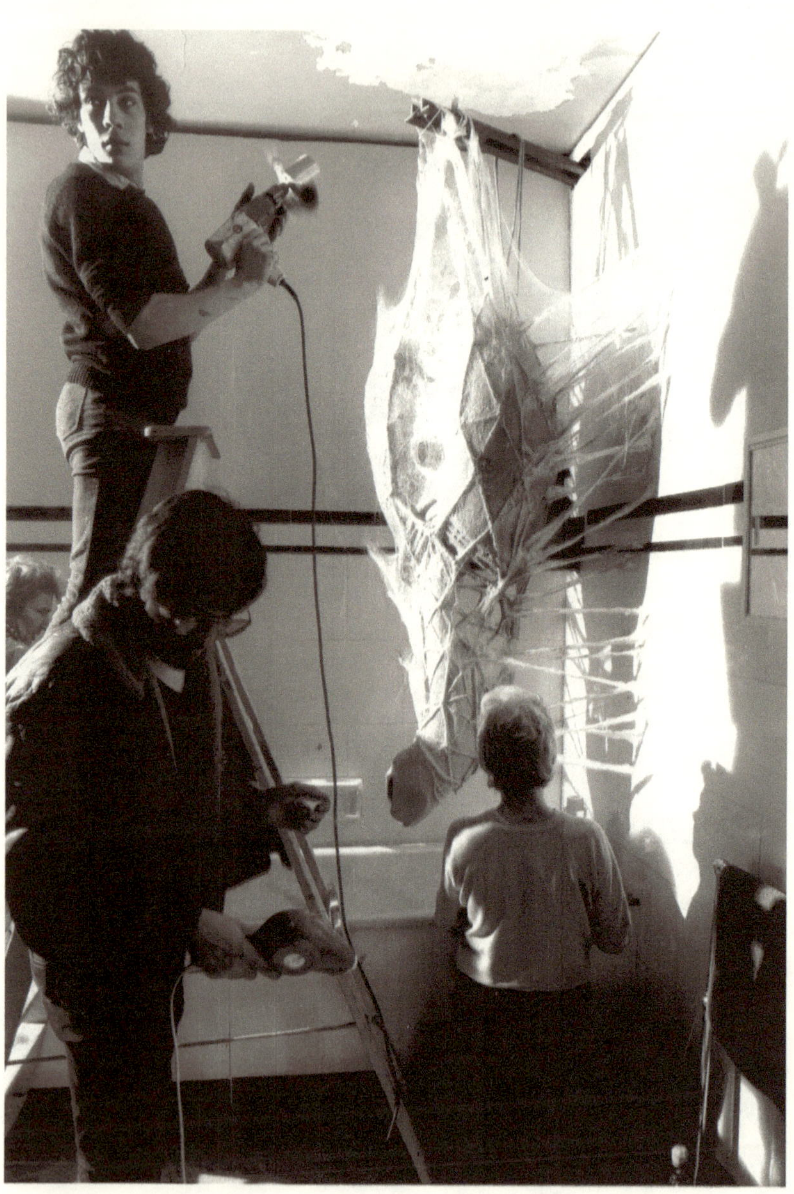

Prepping the coccon scene

Creature attack setup

Harry Bromley Davenport and the creature crew on a very cold night.

Danny Braining (Joe) and Harry Bromley Davenport

Harry Bromley Davenport, Bernice Stegers (Rachel) & Anna Mottram (teacher)

Harry Bromley Davenport and Mark Forstater (producer)

Harry Bromley Davenport directing Simon Nash

Killer toy tank FX

Harry Bromley Davenport, James Crawford (associate producer) and Bernice Stegers (Rachel) in pub after shooting

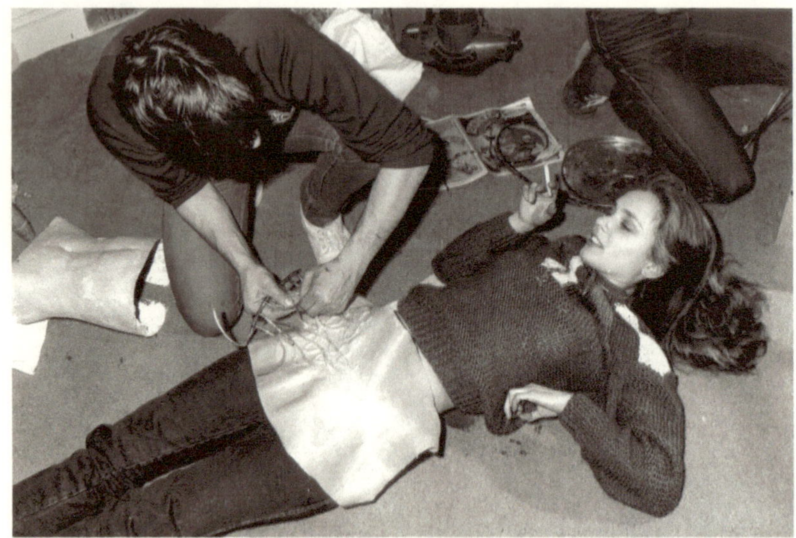

Maryam D'Abo in prosthetics

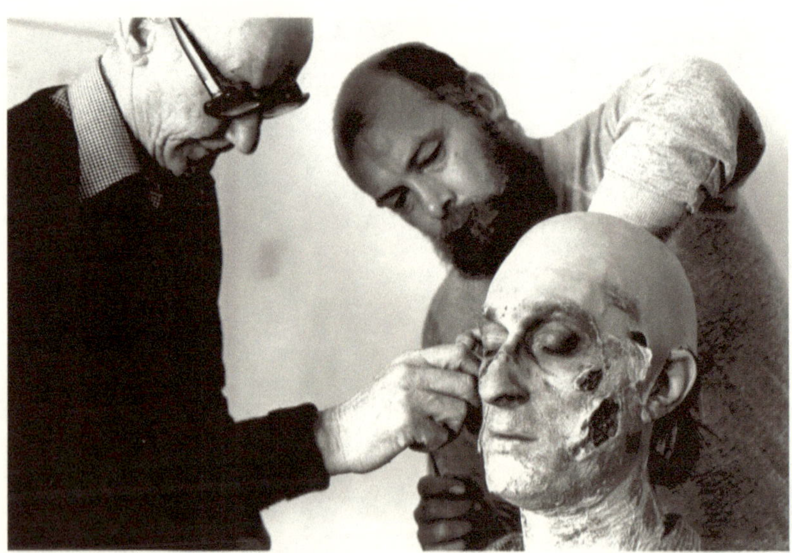

Makeup crew and Philip Sayer (Sam)

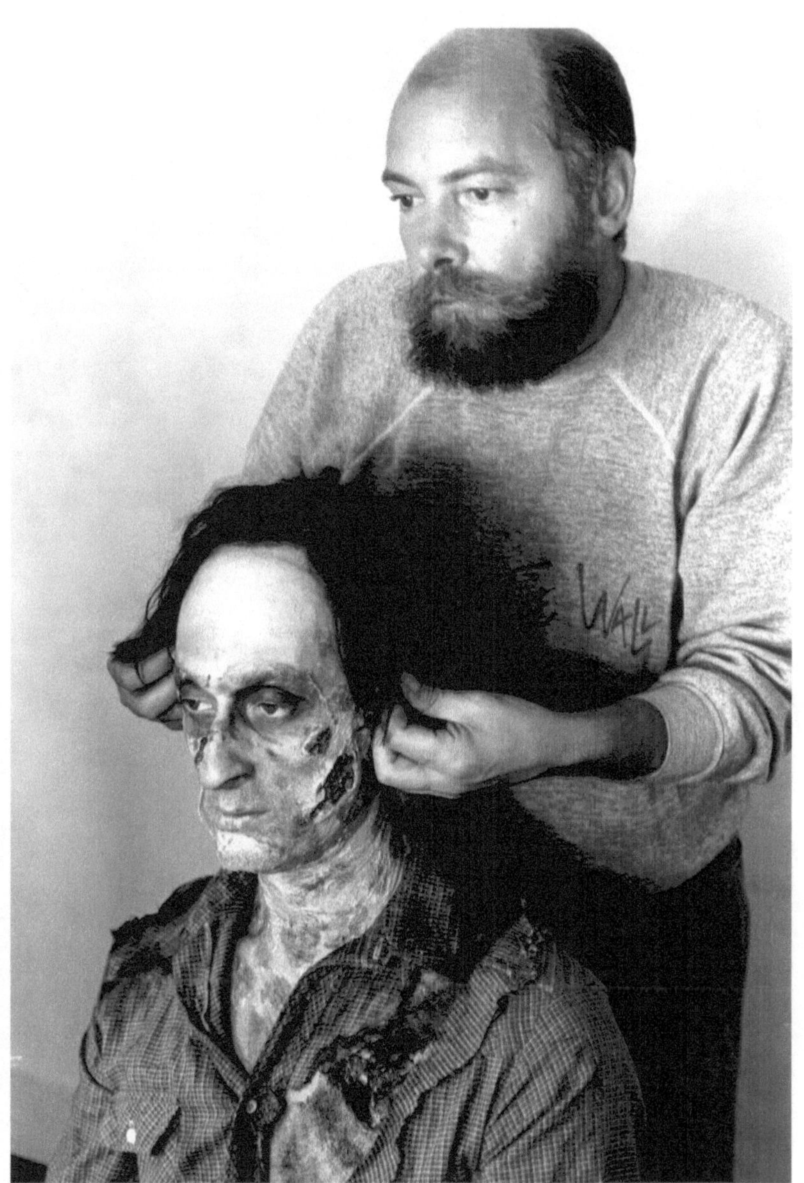

Philip Sayer and Barry Richardson (Hair stylist)

Camera crew & Harry Bromley Davenport in cage protected from live panther

Jake Wright (1st AD), Maryam D'Abo (Analise), David Cardy (Michael) and Harry Bromley Davenport on set

XTRO

DESIGNS AND STORYBOARDS
by Christopher Hobbs

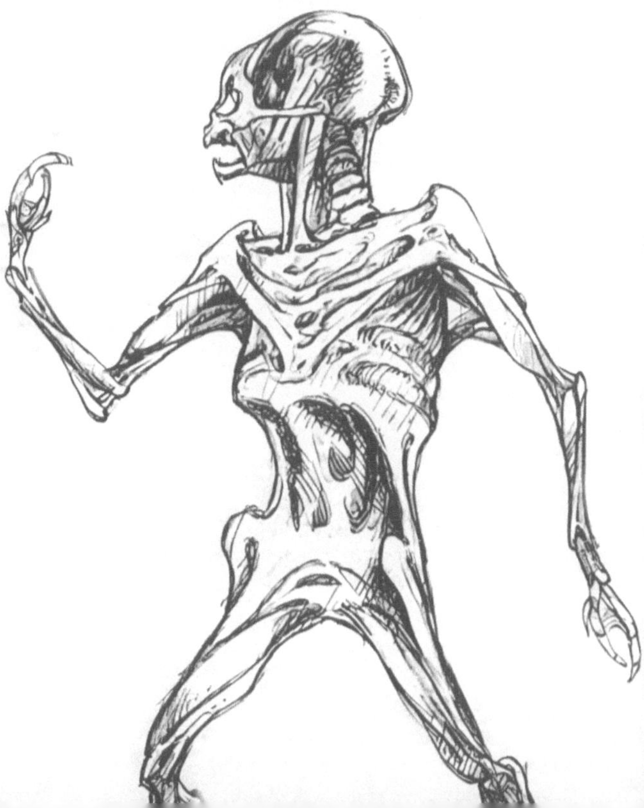

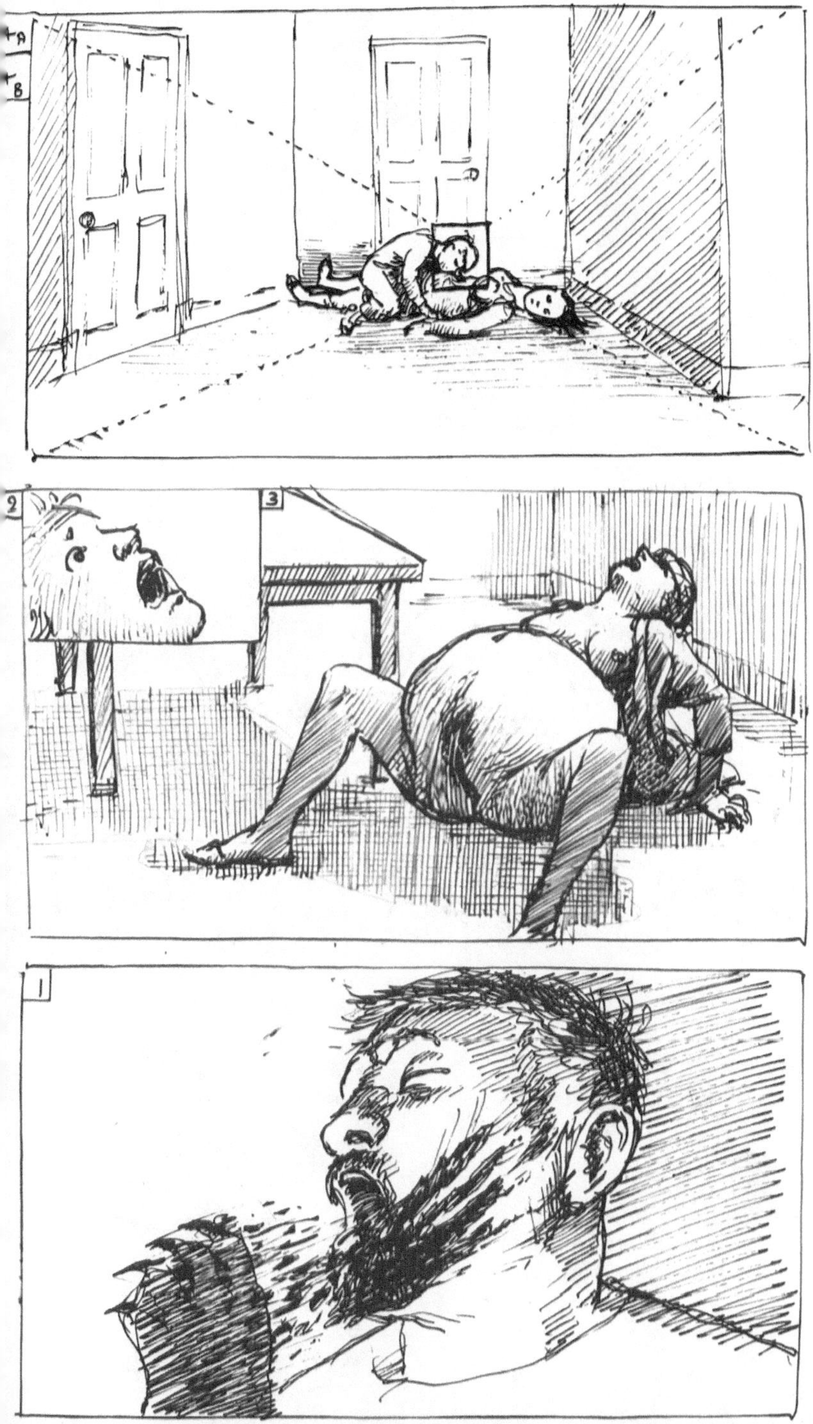

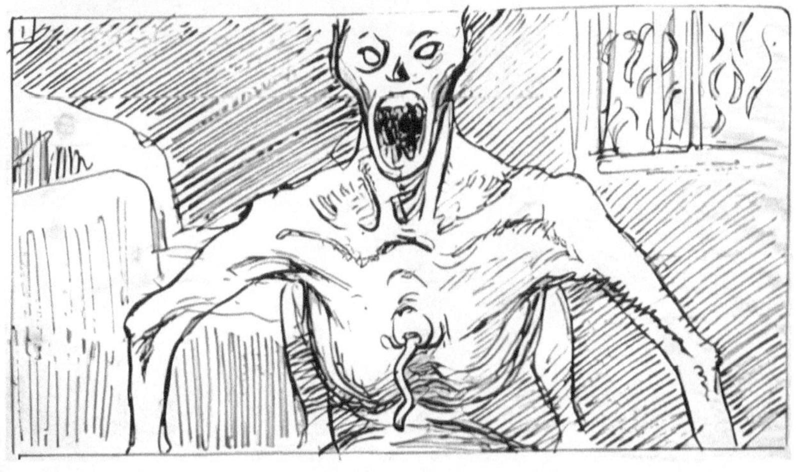

Egg Bucket
in Bath.

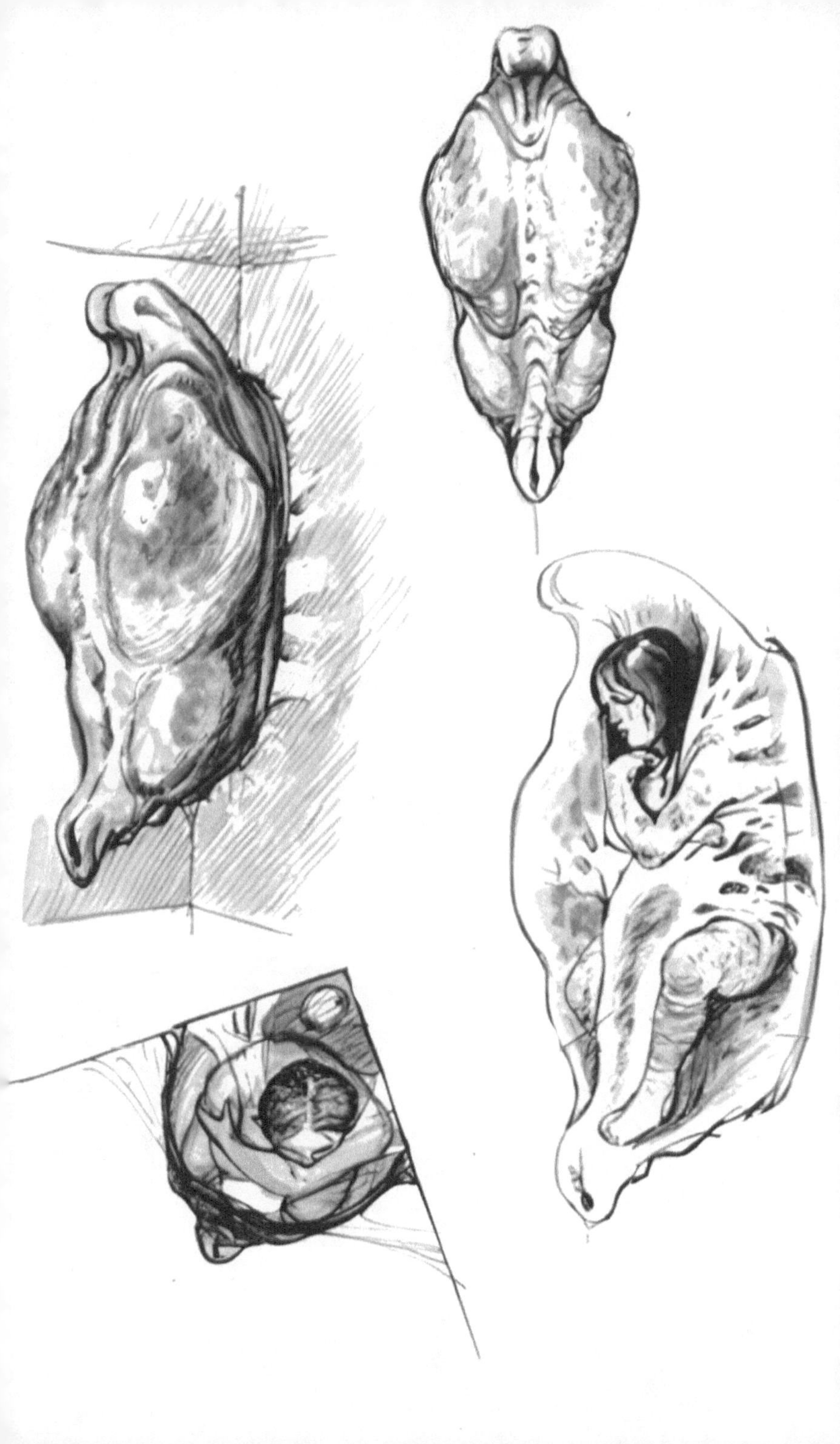

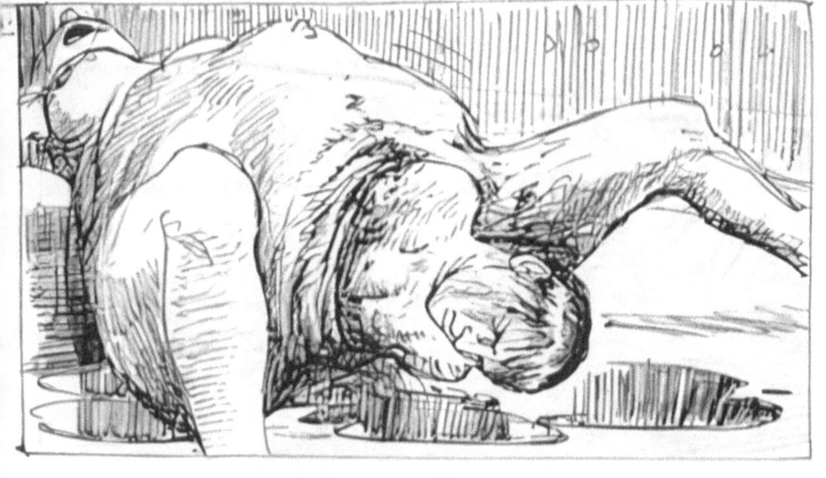

CREATIVE IDEAS DEPARTMENT [ADDIE + AARON SPECIAL DEVELOPMENTS

POSSIBLE SONG FOR JOE AT THIS JUNCTURE

[4]

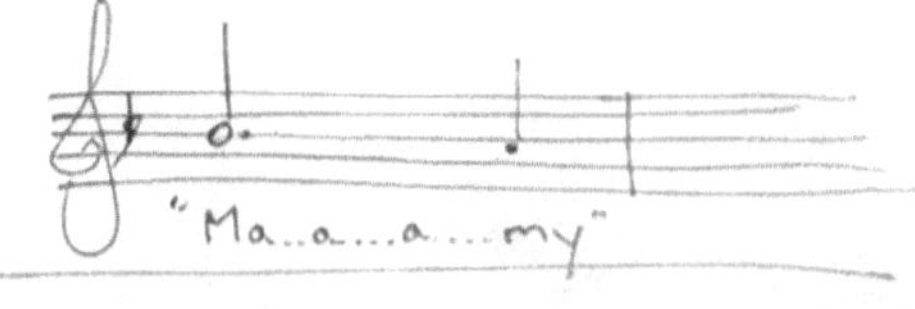

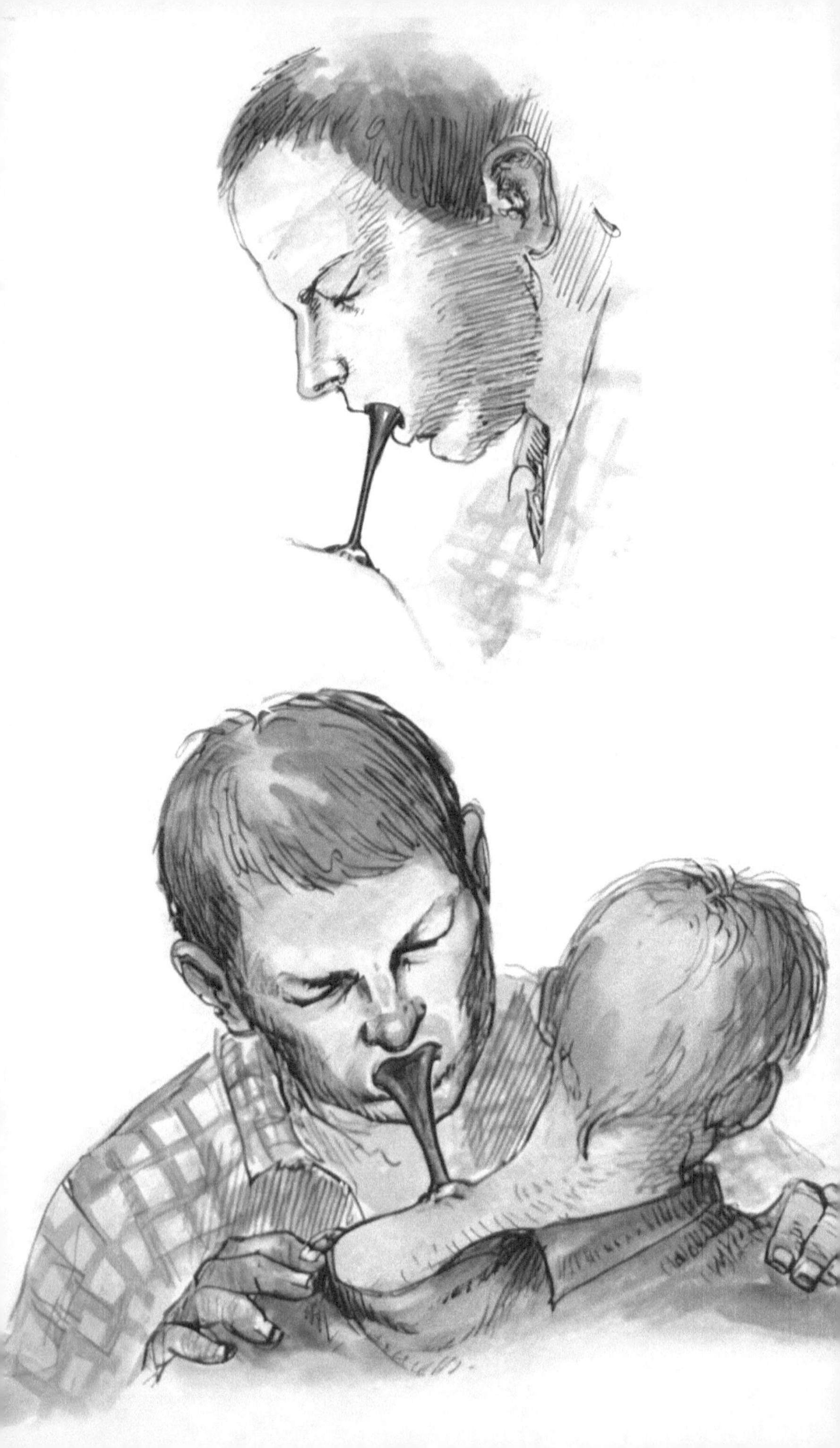

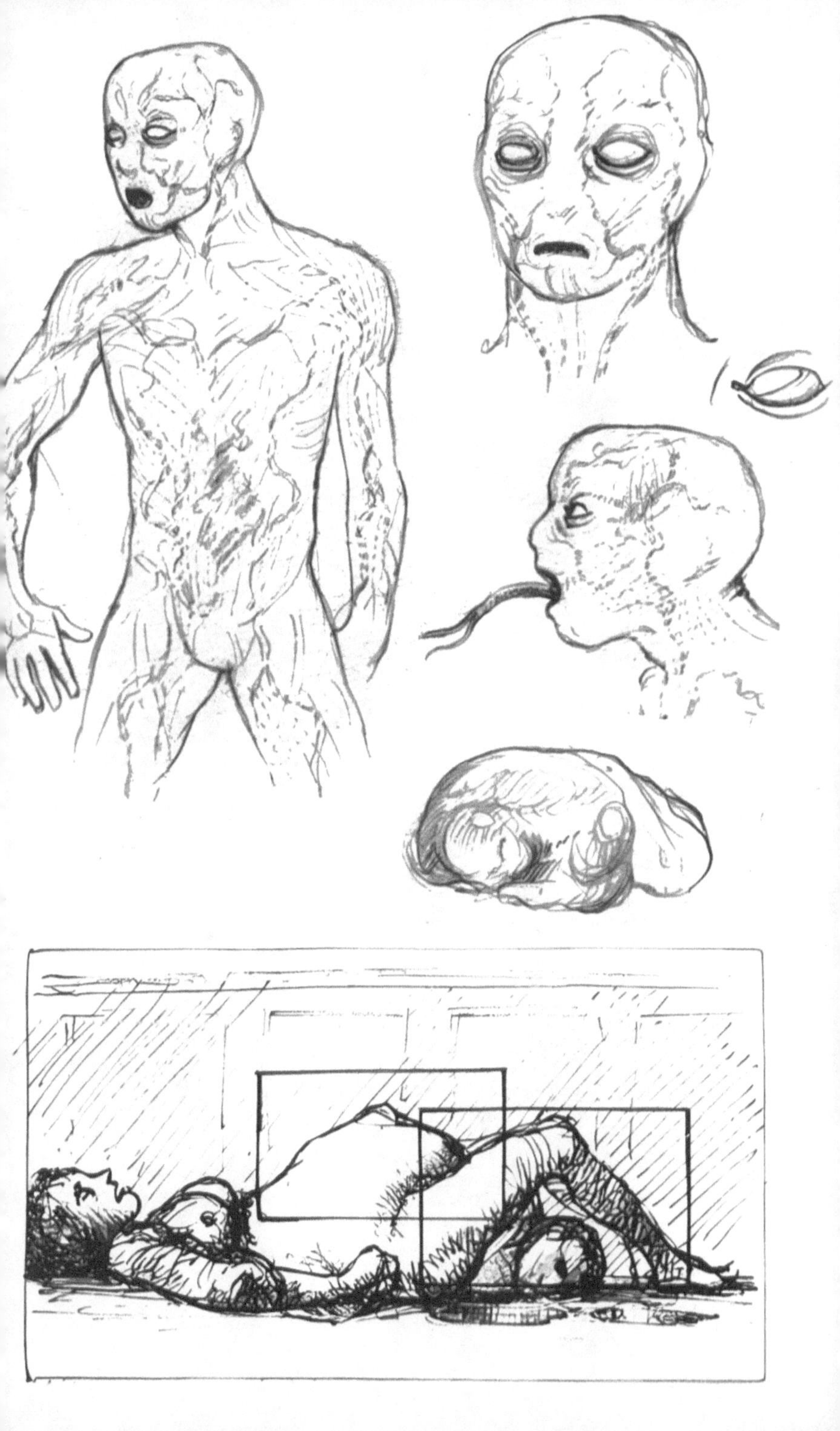

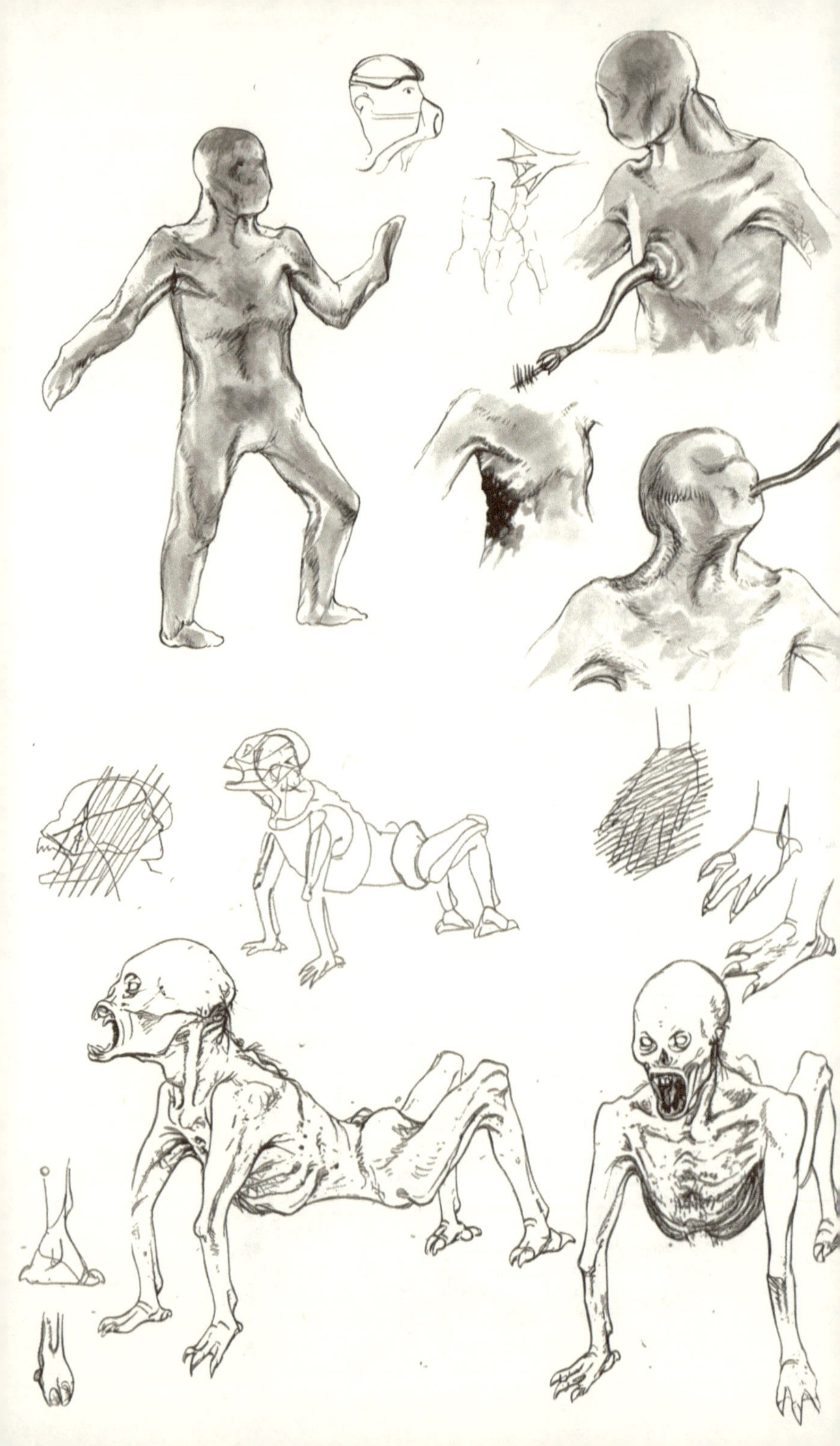

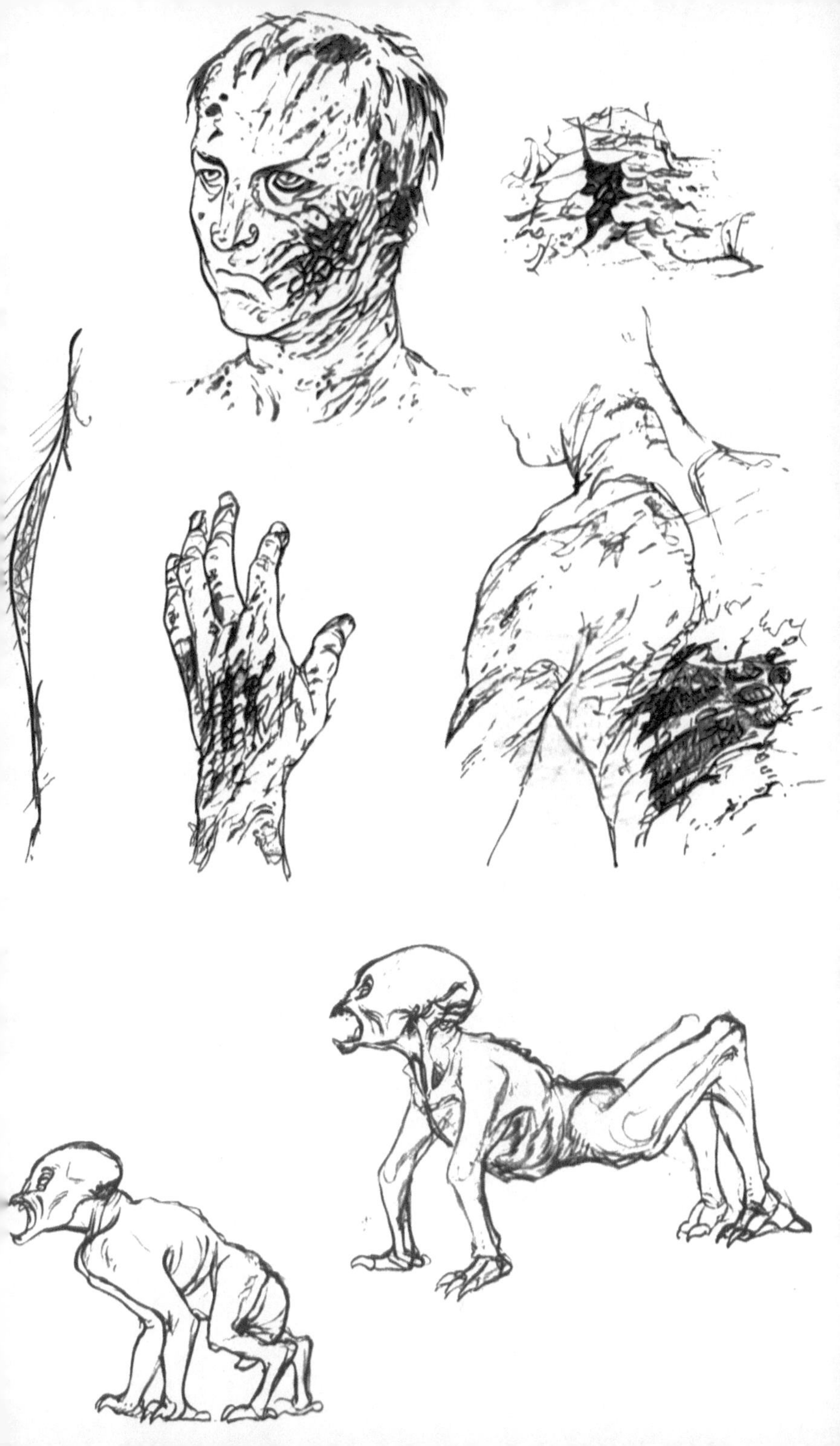

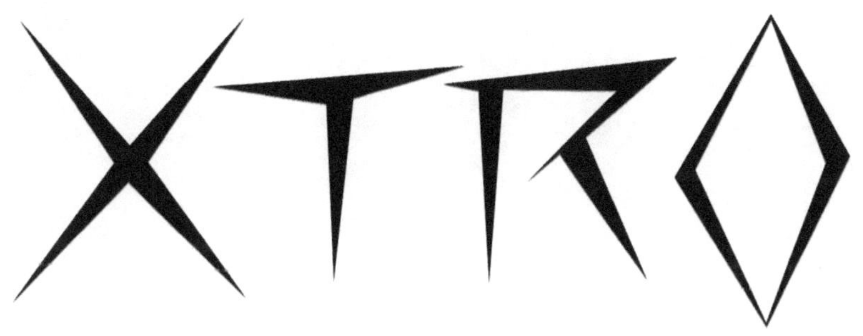

POSTERS, LOBBY CARDS & ADS

CORNE D'OR

GRAND PRIX
DU 13ᵉ FESTIVAL
DE PARIS DU
FILM FANTASTIQUE
ET DE SCIENCE-FICTION

BRUXELLES

stival du film fantastique
et de l'imaginaire.
Grand prix du public
Prix des effets spéciaux.

PORTO

Festival fantastique
Prix des effets spéciaux.

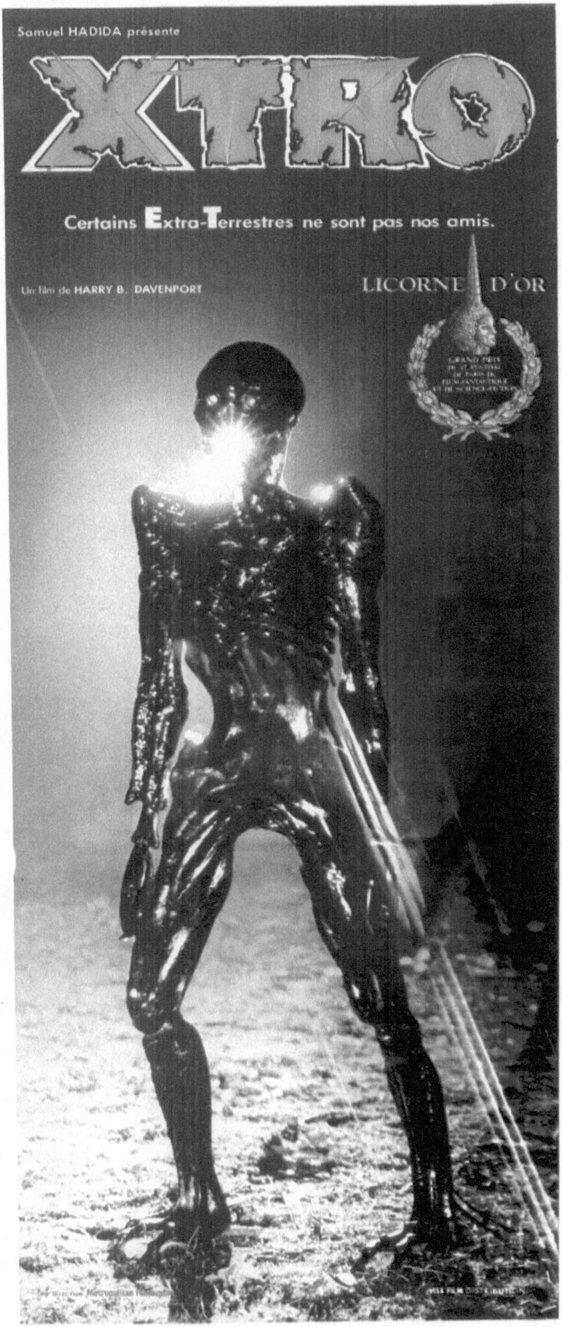

New Realm Entertainments Present
XTRO
18(X)
NOT ALL
EXTRA TERRESTRIALS
ARE FRIENDLY
Executive Producer, Robert Shaye - Producer, Mark Forstater- Director; Harry Bromley Davenport - Screenplay; Iain Cassie, Robert Smith
Based on, original screenplay by, Michel Parry, Harry Bromley Davenport
Music composed and performed by Harry Bromley Davenport
An Amalgamated Film Enterprises Production.

Bearing Powers
of Black Magic..
From Deep Space.
Some extra-terrestrials aren't friendly
XTRO
Starring BERNICE STEGERS PHILIP SAYER SIMON NASH MARYAM D'ABO DANNY BRAININ
Special Effects by NEEFX Speical Effects Makeup by ROBIN GRANTHAM
Director of Photography JOHN METCALFE Associate Producer JAMES CRAWFORD Written by ROBERT SMITH and IAIN CASSIE
Executive producer ROBERT SHAYE Music Composed by HARRY BROMLEY DAVENPORT Special Synthesizer Effects Created by SHELTON LEIGH PALMER
Produced by MARK FORSTATER Directed by HARRY BROMLEY DAVENPORT

THE FAMOUS CULT CLASSIC
MARYAM D'ABO   PHILIP SAYER   BERNICE STEGERS
XTRO
WHEN TONY GROWS UP
HE'S GOING TO BE JUST LIKE DADDY
UNCUT & FULL HD REMASTERED

Samuel HADIDA présente
XTRO
Certains Extra-Terrestres ne sont pas nos amis.
Un film de Harry B DAVENPORT

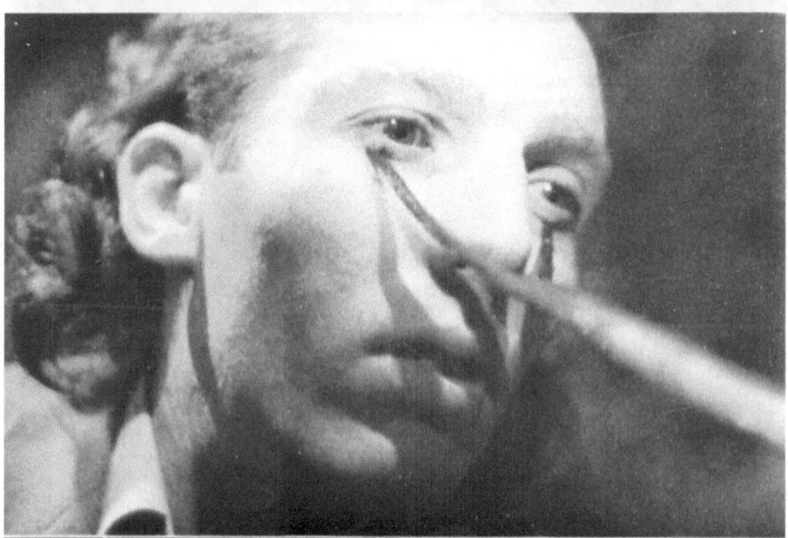

X-TRO
NICHT ALLE
AUSSERIRDISCHEN
SIND FREUNDLICH!

X-TRO
NICHT ALLE AUSSERIRDISCHEN SIND FREUNDLICH!

No todos los extraterrestres son amigos
XTRO
BERNICE STEGERS   PHILIP SAYER   SIMON NASH
MARYAM D'ABO   DANNY BRAININ
Dirección HARRY BROMLEY DAVENPORT   Producto MARK FORSTATER
Productor Ejecutivo ROBERT SHAYE   Productor Asociado JAMES CRAWFORD
Guión ROBERT SMITH y IAIN CASSIE
Director de fotografía JOHN METCALFE   Efectos Especiales TOM HARRIS y FRANCIS COATES
Maquillaje ROBIN GRANTHAM   Música HARRY BROMLEY DAVENPORT
GLOBE
NEW LINE CINEMA

X-TRO
FSK 16
3-DISC LIMITED COLLECTOR'S EDITION

XTRO
DVD VIDEO
GILMON

KULTFILMEN DER BLEV FORBUDT I ENGLAND!
NOT ALL ET'S ARE FRIENDLY...
X-TRO
DVD
15
UNCUT SPECIAL EDITION

X-TRO
NICHT ALLE
AUSSERIRDISCHEN
SIND FREUNDLICH

X-TRO
NICHT ALLE
AUSSERIRDISCHEN
SIND FREUNDLICH

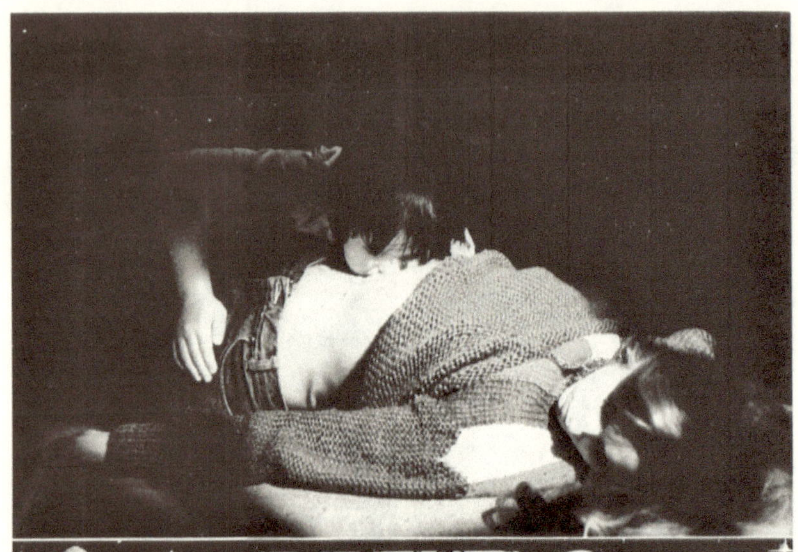

X-TRO
NICHT ALLE AUSSERIRDISCHEN SIND FREUNDLICH!

35th ANNIVERSARY
HD リマスター & ディレクターズカット版
植え付けられる！
地球外生命体の種子
タネ
エクストロ
XTRO

X-TRO
'84
3-DISC LIMITED COLLECTOR'S EDITION

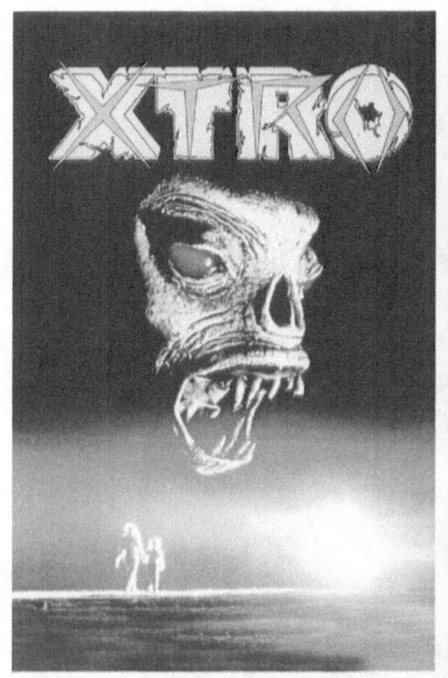

X-TRO

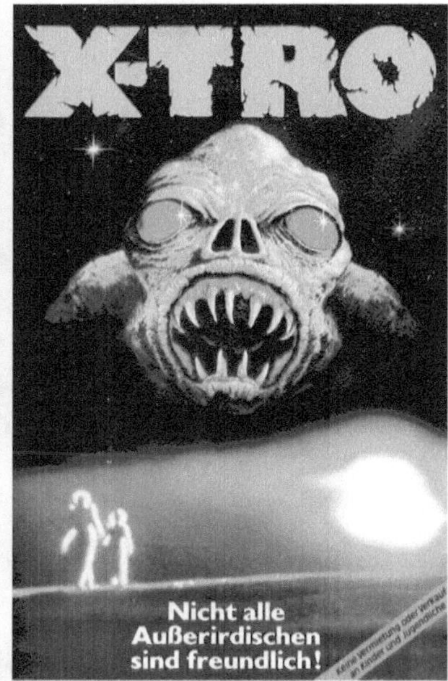

X-TRO
Nicht alle
Außerirdischen
sind freundlich!
Keine Vermietung oder Verkauf an Kinder und Jugendliche

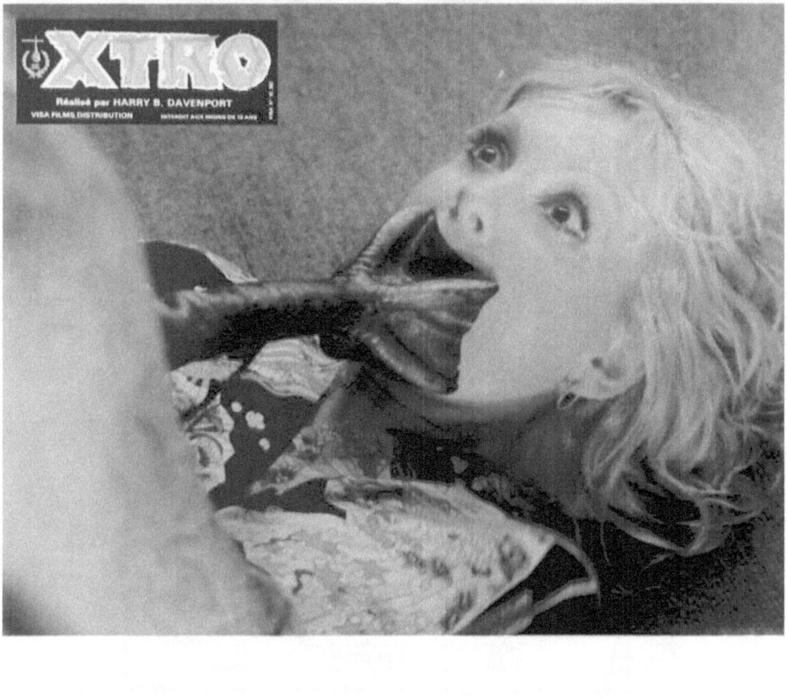

XTRO
Réalisé par HARRY B. DAVENPORT
VISA FILMS DISTRIBUTION
INTERDIT AUX MOINS DE 13 ANS

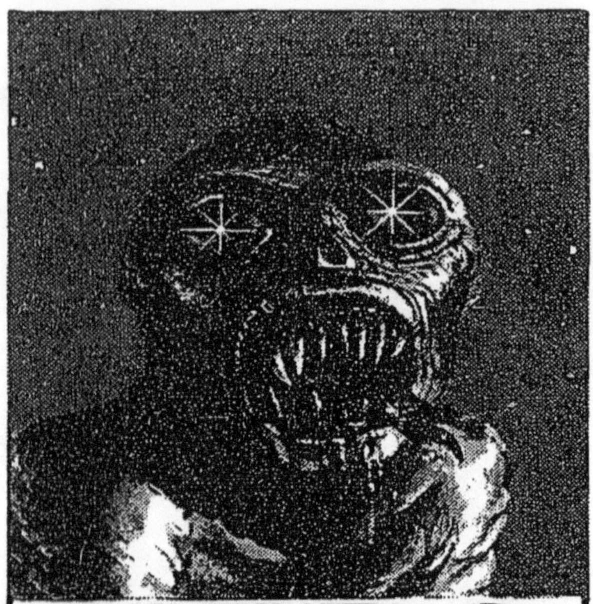

XTRO
Some extra-terrestrials aren't friendly.
Starring BERNICE STEGERS   PHILIP SAYER   MARYAM D'ABO   DANNY BRAININ
Directed by HARRY BROMLEY DAVENPORT   Written by ROBERT SMITH and IAIN CASSIE
Executive Producer ROBERT SHAYE   Producer MARK FORSTATER
R   An Amalgamated Film Enterprises Production From New Line Cinema
STARTS TODAY AT A FLAGSHIP THEATER NEAR YOU

MANHATTAN
RKO CENTURY
RKO NATIONAL
B'WAY AT 44 ST
12 15 2 05 3 55 5 45
7 35 9 25 11 15
LOEWS ORPHEUM
3RD AVE AT 86 ST
1 00 2 40 4 20 6 00
7 40 9 20 11 00
COSMO
116 ST BET LEX & 3RD
ESSEX
GRAND ST OFF ESSEX

BRONX
ALLERTON
CIRCLE
DOVER
KENT
PARADISE
PROSPECT

BROOKLYN
CHOPIN
COMMODORE
DUFFIELD
FORTWAY
HIGHWAY
OCEANA
RIDGEWOOD
RKO KENMORE

QUEENS
ASTORIA
ASTORIA
FLUSHING
QUARTET
FOREST HILLS
MIDWAY
JACKSON HTS.
BOULEVARD
JAMAICA
ROCHDALE
OZONE PARK
CROSS BAY
QUEENS VILLAGE
COMMUNITY

STATEN ISL.
NEW SPRINGVILLE
ISLAND

NASSAU
BALDWIN
RKO BALDWIN
EAST MEADOW
MEADOWBROOK
FRANKLIN SQ.
FRANKLIN
PLAINVIEW
RKO PLAINVIEW
PT. WASHINGTON
TRIPLEX
VALLEY STREAM
SUNRISE MULTIPLEX
WANTAGH
RKO WANTAGH
WESTBURY
WESTBURY DI

SUFFOLK
FARMINGVILLE
COLLEGE PLAZA
HAUPPAUGE
HAUPPAUGE
ISLIP
ISLIP
NESCONSET
SMITHTOWN DI
WEST BABYLON
SOUTH BAY TRIO

WESTCHESTER
MAMARONECK
PLAYHOUSE
NEW ROCHELLE
TOWN
PEEKSKILL
BEACH
YONKERS
PARK HILL

ROCKLAND
NANUET
MOVIES

UPSTATE
KINGSTON
MAYFAIR
MIDDLETOWN
PLAZA

CONNECTICUT
BRIDGEPORT
RKO MERRITT

NEW JERSEY
EAST BRUNSWICK
TURNPIKE DI
EDGEWATER
SHOWBOAT
EDISON
PLAINFIELD INDOOR
FAIR LAWN HY WAY
FREEHOLD ROUTE 9
HACKENSACK
RKO ORITANI
HARRISON
WARNER
IRVINGTON CASTLE
JERSEY CITY STATE
MIDDLETOWN
MOVIES
MONTCLAIR
WELLMONT
MORRISTOWN
COMMUNITY
NEWARK
PARAMOUNT
ORANGE PALACE
PARSIPPANY
TROY HILLS
PATERSON FABIAN
ROCKAWAY TWP.
ROCKAWAY
SAYREVILLE
AMBOY MULTIPLEX
SECAUCUS
LOEWS HARMON COVE
WAYNE
RKO WAYNE

X-TRO
'34
3-DISC LIMITED COLLECTOR'S EDITION

X-TRO
FSK ab 16 freigegeben
'34
3-DISC LIMITED COLLECTOR'S EDITION

EARTH IS THE
HUNTING GROUND.
MAN IS THE
ENDANGERED SPECIES.
EXTRO
RATED R
SHOWS 7:00-9:00
BEECHMONT TWIN
BEECHMONT AT WARWICK
874-1991

X-TRO
NICHT ALLE
AUSSERIRDISCHEN
SIND FREUNDLICH!

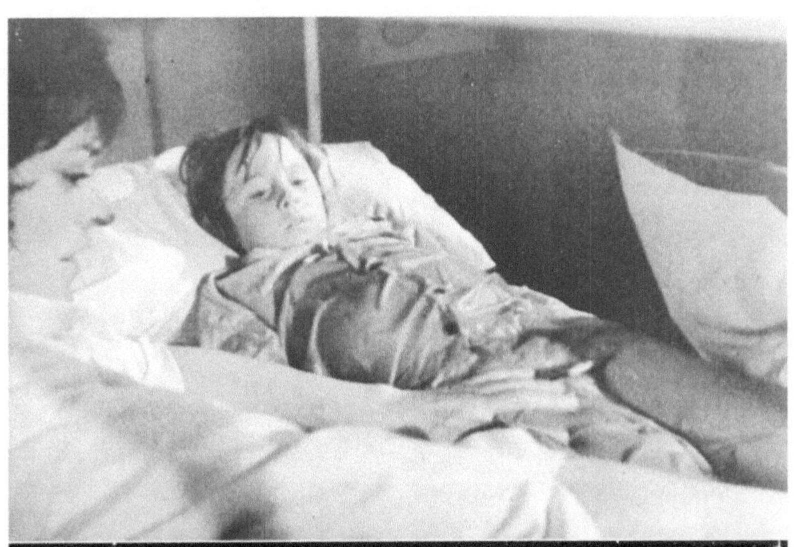

SNEAK PREVIEW TONIGHT AT 7:30

X-TRO
NICHT ALLE AUSSERIRDISCHEN SIND FREUNDLICH

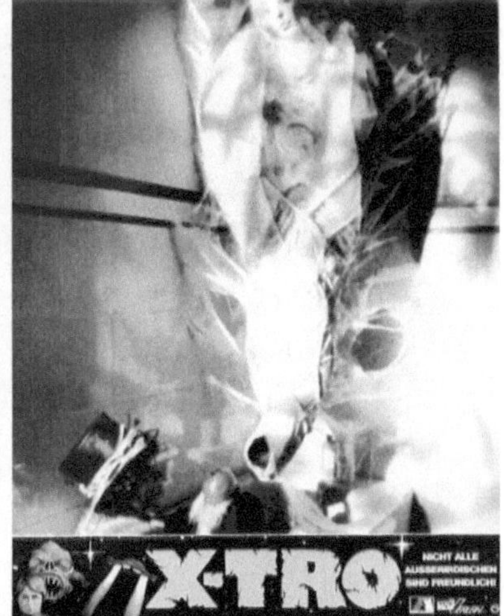
X-TRO
NICHT ALLE AUSSERIRDISCHEN SIND FREUNDLICH

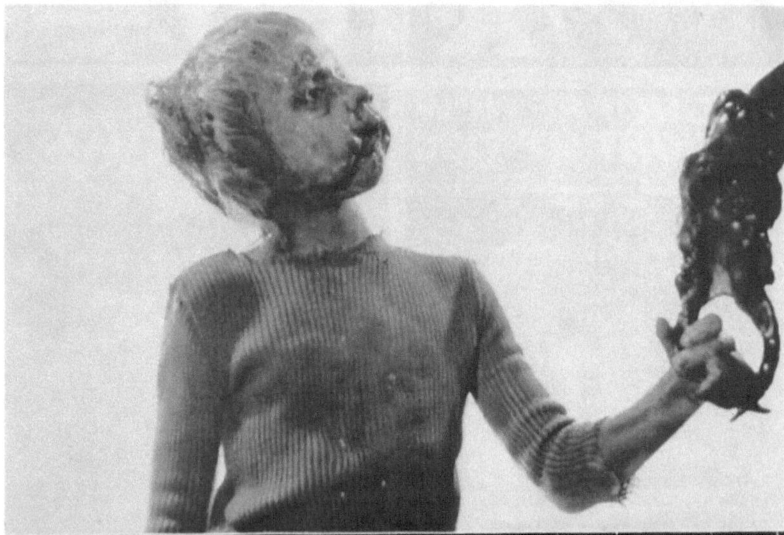

X-TRO
NICHT ALLE AUSSERIRDISCHEN SIND FREUNDLICH!

XTRO
THIS ALIEN IS PURE EVIL

"XTRO (ek'strō) n. Scientific jargon for extraterrestrial creature."
First it will control the planet...
XTRO
AT CANNES
HOTEL MARTINEZ 08.01.01
New Line International Releasing Inc.
Principal photography completed. Available in August.
Special Screening of 30 minutes Production Reel
May 17 ... 2:30 pm (14h30)
PALAIS Salle F

GRAND PRIX AU FESTIVAL DU FILM FANTASTIQUE DE PARIS - 1983
L'HORRIBLE INVASION COMMENCE...
XTRO

KULT-KLASSIKER
UNGESCHNITTEN
XTRO

Bearing Powers
of Black Magic..
From Deep Space.
Some extra-terrestrials aren't friendly
XTRO
Starring BERNICE STEGERS PHILIP SAYER SIMON NASH MARYAM D'ABO DANNY BRAININ
Special Effects by NEEFX Special Effects Makeup by ROBIN GRANTHAM
Director of Photography JOHN METCALFE Associate Producer JAMES CRAWFORD Written by ROBERT SMITH and IAIN CASSIE
Executive producer ROBERT SHAYE Music Composed by HARRY BROMLEY DAVENPORT Special Synthesizer Effects Created by SHELTON LEIGH PALMER
Produced by MARK FORSTATER Directed by HARRY BROMLEY DAVENPORT

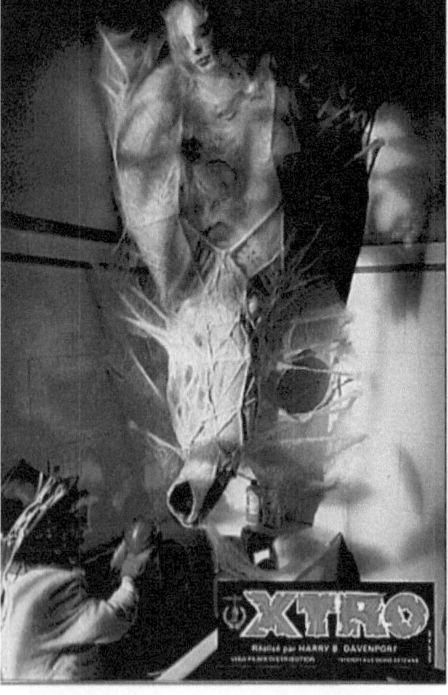
XTRO
Réalisé par HARRY B. DAVENPORT

NOT ALL EXTRATERRESTRIALS
ARE FRIENDLY.
XTRO

XTRO
Pal Mal
Video Tudu

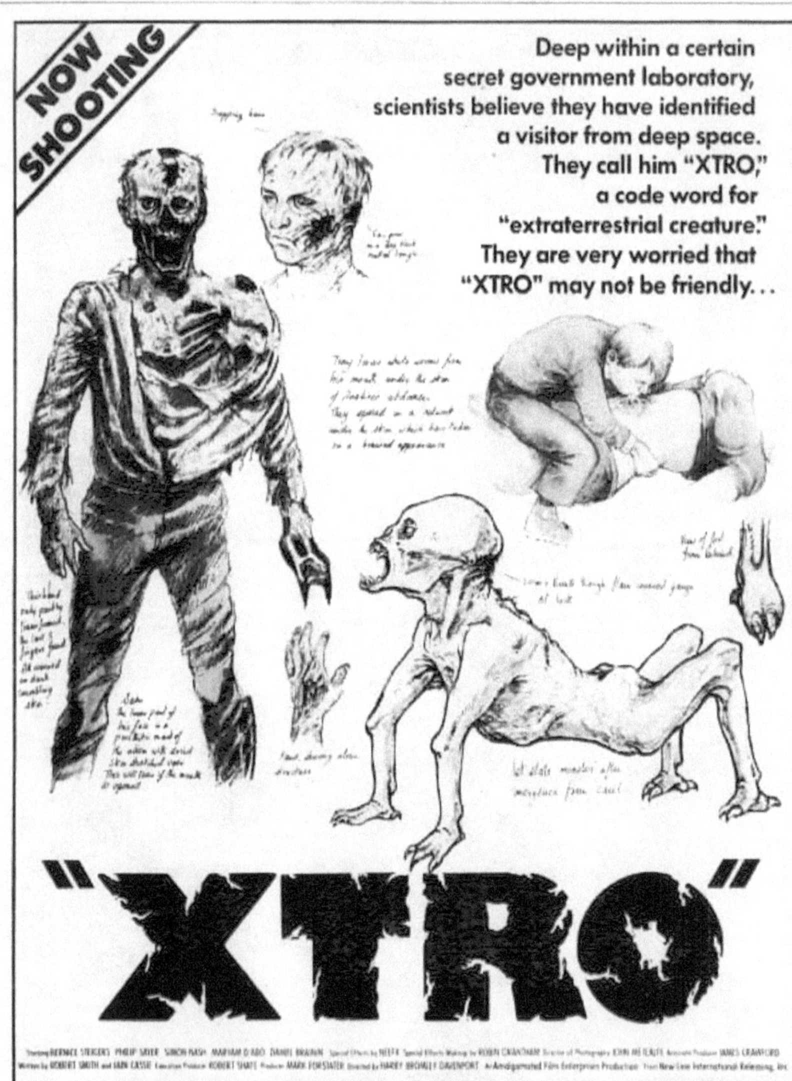

NOW SHOOTING
Deep within a certain secret government laboratory, scientists believe they have identified a visitor from deep space. They call him "XTRO," a code word for "extraterrestrial creature." They are very worried that "XTRO" may not be friendly...
"XTRO"
Starring BERNICE STENGERS PHILIP SAYER SIMON NASH MARYAM D'ABO DANNY BRAININ Special Effects by NEETA Special Effects Make-up by ROBIN GRANTHAM Director of Photography JOHN METCALFE Associate Producer JAMES CRAWFORD Written by ROBERT SMITH and IAIN CASSIE Executive Producer ROBERT SHAYE Producer MARK FORSTATER Directed by HARRY BROMLEY DAVENPORT An Amalgamated Film Enterprises Production From New Line International Releasing, Inc.
AMERICAN FILM MARKET
Stanley Dudelson / Robert Shaye
Rooms 1025 & 1027   THE WESTWOOD PLAZA HOTEL   Tel. (213) 475-5576
New Line International Releasing Inc.
853 Broadway, New York, New York 10003 (212) 674-7460   Telex: 426407 NLCC   Cable: Newlinezin

Harry Bromley Davenport and producer Mark Forstater reunite for the first time since the original XTRO to create XTRO – The Big One, the fourth installment in the series. This new chapter follows an alien invasion unfolding simultaneously with "The Big One," the catastrophic Los Angeles earthquake.

XTRO
THE BIG ONE

Harry Bromley Davenport in Hollywood working on FX shots